REFLECTIONS ALONG THE WAY

There he is in the woods. There again looking up at stars.

Here are poetic reflections spanning twenty and more years. Jim Casey thinking, asking, guessing, wander-wondering relentlessly in exploration and searches among the trees and up into the night sky and deep into the atoms and far out to the cosmos and then returning again and again to his beloved Hudson River Valley and its Storm King and its trees. He loves the trees as teachers, and all along the paths in his forests — at foot around him and also inside his head — pop up delightful echoing phrases of Church Latin as rich bits of meaning playing out of his past. Full of reflections through open questions, often without answers, on the wonder that is life.

Michael Whelan
Author of *After God*

Here are more than a century of pages from a man who tells us how he's tried to find himself in Nature, in God, and other modes of thought. These are his reflections about the process and what he found in the places he looked.

The poems and poetic expressions show an earnestness of quest and I am sure the astute reader will want to engage the author with questions.

Reflections invites each reader to go off and jot down his or her assessments of life and to return with gifts for the community at large.

Dennis Sullivan
Le Jardin de La Grande Chartreuse

REFLECTIONS ALONG THE WAY

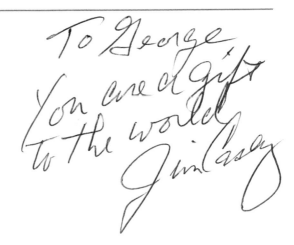

To George,
You are a gift
to the world
Jim Casey

JAMES CASEY

In Paradisum Press
Putnam Valley, New York

REFLECTIONS ALONG THE WAY

In Paradisum Press
12 Lookout Pass
Putnam Valley, New York 10579
inparadisum@optonline.net

For information contact:
In Paradisum Press,
Contact the author at: inparadisum@optonline.net

Library of Congress Control Number: 2018905456

ISBN-13: 978-0-692-11728-6

PHOTO CREDITS:

Cover photos by Kristin Casey.

The front cover photo is of the Bonnefont Cloister. The back cover is of the Cuxa Cloister, both located in the Cloisters, a branch of the Metropolitan Museum of Art in New York City.

For
Brian, Kristin,
James, and Patrick

The music you create

In love with the spirits of your soul

Is an invitation for the world to sing.

Authors Note

What are found in these pages are personal reflections of the author that span a period of approximately twenty-five years. The reader may notice what appears to be an evolution of thought. Indeed, over that period my thinking has wandered down many paths and I hope that will continue to be the case as I move closer to a deeper understanding of the way things are. I am certain of one thing however, certainty is elusive. So reader beware, what you read here should be taken *cum grano salis*.

CONTENTS

Introduction	1
Grave Remarks	9
Forgiveness	10
Expectations	11
A Walk In The Woods	12
Alone in the Adirondacks	14
Swan and a Boy	17
A Child's Plea	18
Joyous Symphony	19
Fools Work	20
Light of Life	21
Stars of Wonder	22
Journey	23
Crows Delight	25
Integrity	26
Recovery Area	29
AΩ Alpha and Omega	30
The Light of Love	31
Prayer	32
Complementarity of Opposites	33
On Wiseass Remarks	34
The Intelligence of the Universe	35
Creative Energy	36

Just Us	38
The Learned Man	39
Peace	40
Harmony	41
Silence, the Gateway to Self-Knowledge	42
Gift to the World	43
Non-attachment to the Wisdom of Others	44
A Mighty Mountain	45
Reflection on An Evening Prayer	47
A Christmas Thought	48
Spring	49
Summer	50
Via Dolorosa	51
Love's Embrace	53
The Candle of the Innocents	54
Eternal Are The Ghosts	57
Light	58
Looking for Truth	60
Heaven	62
Ordinary Things	64
The God Idea	67
Heart of Love	68
A Jewel of a Story	69
The Path to Peace	70
From the Stars to the Stars	71
Shining Stars	73

A World Illuminated 74

That 75

A Walk in Amity Forest 77

Gratitude 78

A Paradise Mind 79

The Sounds of Silence 80

The Robin Visits 82

In Silence Watching 83

Wonder at Wondering 84

Sophia 86

De Colores A Song I Sing 88

Celebrating a Life 90

A Numinous Web 92

Kuroki's Garden 94

Poetic Experience 95

My Grandson By My Side 96

Love 98

Lone Star Lonely No More 100

Human Spirit 102

Haiku 103

My Daimon 106

Creation 107

Love Remains 109

What is Life? 111

Noise 114

A Dream 116

Keys to the Kingdom   117

The Word of The Lord   118

The Face of Storm King Mountain   119

Mary   120

The Robin Returns   121

Trees   122

The Hermit in Silence Sits   124

Self   125

Self a Dream   126

On Solitude   128

Ancestral Ghosts Exorcised   130

Contrasting Stories at Christmas   131

Christmas Story   132

L'Histoire de Noël   133

Lonely   135

Something Big   136

Alone   138

Awesome   139

The World We Think We Know   140

Snow Fall   141

Seed to Soul   142

Rachel Weeping For Her Children   144

I Wonder About The World   146

What Have We Done To The Spirit   148

What Beautiful Snow Can Do   149

Love Mountain   150

Gratitude   152

A Spring Greeting   153

God Doesn't Draw Straight Lines   154

A Stellar Development   156

TESS   158

Firefighters Obey The Highest Law   159

Convenient Labels   161

The Demilitarized Zone   162

Acknowledgements   163

About The Author   164

Introduction

We do not see reality. It is hidden by the assumption that our perception is correct. We construct the world we see based on our evolutionary inheritance. Our perception of the world evolved more concerned with survival than with accurate representation of reality. It is "our world" that we see.

Over time we shape our view of the world through our interaction with "our world," which in turn shapes the world we see and how we act in it. We do not shape our worldview in isolation. We are complicit with others in "our world," specifically with family, friends and associates, including teachers, religious guides, and employers. The broader culture in which we are swimming and to which we all contribute is almost unseen, though it is part of "our world" and forms a loop with us of reciprocal influence.

We are like fish in a pond sucking in water. The water contains contributions from all the fish in the pond. It may not be clean water, but it is their water, the only water they know. They are thinking this is reality, as if this is just the way the world is until one day one of them takes a flying leap above the surface of the water and sees a world beyond imagination. As we can imagine the report of a revised worldview might well be met with skepticism and ridicule.

There are many "ponds" across the globe, cultures with stories passed down through the ages from one generation to the next. When the world was smaller, these "ponds" were separated by geographical boundaries. Stories developed within each of them with limited impact from other cultures.

As a species, we have been telling ourselves stories ever since we climbed down from the trees. We humans seem to have a propensity for them. Stories tell us of our connectedness to family, tribe, nation, and the world. They have shaped our understanding of who we are and what we are capable of achieving. Our self-identity is related to them.

We have inherited highly imaginative ancient stories that place the human in a cosmic context. They speculate on origins, describing through primitive cosmologies the movement from chaos to cosmos. Within that context they explain the relationship of the specifically human to the vast world that they could see, which included the mystery of the forces and powers in that world that were far greater than their own. We are still at it today. Cosmologists have recently begun to speculate about a story beyond the cosmic unity of a single universe to the possibility of a multiverse.

Some of these ancient stories, which seem to have developed in most, if not all cultures, reflect wonder and awe at the cosmic mystery that lies before the human mind. Their world was full of mystery, wonder and fear in face of the uncertainties surrounding them. The stories express the need to make sense of the world, the significance we humans have in relation to it and what that means for how we should act. The stories served to pass on that wisdom to their children and their children's children.

The process of arriving at these stories was achieved in small communities by dialogue eventually leading to consensus. But the stories were shaped by limited observation of the world, much of it inaccurate. They did not have the information about the world that we have today. Survival needs played an important part in how communities perceived the world and that perception was reflected in the stories they told about it.

Until the discovery of writing, these stories were passed down by word of mouth from generation to generation. They were dynamic stories, shaped within an historical context by the participation of the individuals in the community. The stories were coherent, if not accurate, in the way they portrayed the world. Coherence seemed to imply truth. Down through the generations the story was edited based on contemporary understanding reflecting current events that impacted the community. The stories evolved in a dynamic process in relatively small communities for most of human history.

However, since the invention of writing, one can wonder if the same dynamic process of developing the communal worldview, by involving the individuals in the community, has continued. I suggest that the written story, as well as, the increased size of communities discouraged, to some extent, active individual participation in editing and reshaping the story within the ongoing historical context. This enabled many people to become apathetic in thinking and wondering about their world. After all, they had the story. They yielded it to 'story keepers' to whom they gave the authority to both guard the story and speak 'the word of the Lord' as written. In this process the story becomes 'his story,' a history told to the community rather than shaped by the community.

One can only wonder about the quality of the story as passed down through the ages. To what extent were 'story keepers' concerned about their position? Was there a tendency to protect their authority by dogmatizing the story, thus inhibiting participation by others in editing it? As they passed the story from generation to generation did they provide the next generation with the caveat that the wisdom being transmitted just might not be wisdom? Such wisdom might encourage the next generation to question the tradition in such a way as to root out any error in the story.

Questioning the story did happen, of course. Some individuals risked life and limb to stand apart and challenge the status quo.

A question for today is: to what extent do we see ourselves and live out our lives based on a worldview informed largely by an ancient inherited story? Limited knowledge of the cosmos shaped these ancient stories. Do largely inherited beliefs and assumptions about the world impact how we understand ourselves and live out our lives? This raises another question: are we now in a new axial age between stories where former certainties are questioned while new ideas have not yet coalesced to form a new story that informs us of who we are, what our relationship is to the Universe and that addresses the question of meaning in life?

Among other attempts to question tradition, the Enlightenment of the seventeenth and eighteenth centuries, with its emphasis on reason, opened the door to questioning. It has given us additional wisdom with the scientific method to keep the door always open to new possibilities. Future data may improve what we think we know. We may know some information with a high degree of certainty, but (probably) never with absolute certainty. Developing humility with respect to what we know is added wisdom. It behooves us to think that we just might be wrong.

In the past century science has opened the door much wider by increased discoveries. Both cosmic evolution, understood as the origin and development of the universe, and biological evolution, understood as the origin, development and diversity of life provide us with current information far richer than we would ever have imagined.

This new knowledge gives us the opportunity to create a new story. It can be, I believe, a story that unifies humanity with all our diversity, one that transcends the limited cultural stories that historically have divided us. We can create a story that informs us as individuals with meaning and purpose. This story could move toward a cosmic view. A story in which we understand that we are not some insignificant entity inside a finished universe, but rather that we are the very Universe itself in process of becoming, always becoming. Each of us is a link in the chain that will shape its future. An awesome responsibility!

If we should fail to transcend our local cultural stories will that raise the specter of Carl Sagan's postulation that we might just become another "terminated experiment in the process of evolution"?

The reflections in this book are my ponderings over recent years. I wish I had recorded in writing my thoughts throughout my life. For sure, they are written in my memory, but memory is not like a video recording of an event. The story I have inscribed there has been edited continuously, shaped by life experiences interpreted by the story already written in my mind.

Overall, the reflections recorded here include my wonder at life and the questions I have asked myself along the way. They are only a snippet of that process and though I wrote many in poetic form, I make no claim at being a poet. I will leave that label for others to decide.

I must say that I have enjoyed the struggle to capture in words the wonder that is beyond my words to describe. I can only hope that these musings will spark an interest in others to wonder about "what the heck is he trying to say" and that personal engagement will bring along with it the joy and delight that I have encountered along the way. That process of questioning over time has challenged the story that I inherited.

I am most grateful to teachers I have encountered along this journey. They have inspired me to break the chains that bind and risk insecurity to engage what life presents. Those teachers were encountered outside the classroom as well as within. They taught me by the very lives they lived and continue to live. Engagement with them along the way has challenged me to live well, to remain "strong in will / To strive, to seek, to find, and not to yield."1 "They shall shine as stars for all eternity."2

---

1 The last line and a quarter from Alfred Lord Tennyson's poem "Ulysses."
2 **Meditations** by John Baptist de La Salle, edited by Augustine Loes, FSC and Francis Huether, FSC. Lasallian Publications, 1994, reprinted 2007. P 471, meditation 208.2. See also, Dn 12:3.

REFLECTIONS

JAMES CASEY

Grave Remarks

Brother,
Fellow traveler,
Blessed journeyman,
Having unlocked the portal
To that precious azure land,
Heritage to us all,
You stand face to face with Truth.

We, who skirt the perimeter walls,
Grab a glance perchance,
As face to face with earth we stand,
Yet unable to see beyond the dirt
To know that of this stuff we are made,
And each of us apart does not the tale tell.
Sun and earth is mother-father to us all
And beyond that, Truth in mystery lies.

In death you transport treasures from afar
Like the Wise Men of old bearing gifts of gold.

To us who have eyes to see,
It is the key to that precious azure land,
Held firmly in our hand.
We get to unlock the portal of our choice,
For the very same key,
That opens the gates of Heaven
Opens the gates of Hell.

The sign above the door reads,
"The only real death
Is the death we die every day by not living."
And the key is in our hands.
What a gift! And that's the truth.
Thank you, Brother.

3/18/2005

Forgiveness

In the shower
I understood:
forgiveness is
a greater gift
to the forgiver
than the forgiven.

To forgive is
to let go of the past,
to untie the bonds,
to be available to the present.

Commentary

This poem reminds me of the story of the two monks walking through the woods. They come upon a young woman fearful of crossing the river. The one monk picks her up and carries her across. On the other side the monks continue on their walk in silence, one sullen the other enjoying the walk in the woods. The sullen monk begins to berate his brother: "You know, back there you broke the Rule. We have promised never to touch a woman. How could you do that?" The monk responded: "I carried her across the river and put her down. I see you are still carrying her."

6/16/1994

Expectations

Riding home from work
Revelation
Sign on a truck:
"It Never Ends."

Expectations!
Why do I expect it to end?
To create my own disappointment,
Terror?

Perceptions!
Anxiety, fear, terror.
In reality?
In my mind?

Who's in charge here, anyway?
It's in the expectations.
Que sera, sera!
Create contentment.

Expect nothing!

7/9/1994

A Walk In The Woods

On a walk in the woods
Air
Cool
Soft

A slow deep breath
Ah

Smells
Damp
Earth
Rotting

Damp earth rotting

A slow deep breath
Ah *Exultate jubilate* 3

Trees
Leaves fall
Corrode

Millennia
The earth is built up

Silence
Reflection
Memento Homo
Quia pulvis es
Et in pulverem reverteris 4

---

3 *Exultate jubilate* is Latin for "rejoice and be glad." It is a motet by Mozart, K 165. The music is pure joy, as is the smell of the forest floor.
4 The translation from Latin is: "Remember, man, you are dust and unto dust you will return." See Gen 3:19 "For you

In the silence of the forest
Truth
Of the earth earthy

As the leaf
I too will fall
Corrode

May my contribution
With the same simple integrity be

Earth
Built up
All one
Forever and ever
Amen

8/29/1994

---

are dirt, and to dirt you shall return." The Roman Catholic Church
speaks these words in the Ash Wednesday liturgy while placing
ashes on the foreheads of the faithful.

Alone in the Adirondacks

On the first day, I went to Marcy Dam. I'm not sure why, but I always seem drawn to it. I shortly pass through the hemlocks, and immediately the smells, and light, streaming through the branches, reawaken memories of previous years, and the joyous exhilaration of passing through this place.

I know the forest is God's gift to the stressed. I feel it every time I enter. There is peace here, and truth to be found in the silence. "Come to me, all you who labor and are burdened, and I will give you rest,"5 it says, "For I will refresh the weary soul; every soul that languishes I will replenish."6

As I continue on, as through a green tunnel, I hear the voice of Marcy Brook calling out to me, at first gently, and then with authority, saying, "Come, rest by my side and listen." I rest briefly, listen, and gratefully anticipate what is just ahead. Shortly, I see the light at the end of the tunnel, and break out into the majesty of Marcy Dam. Oh wondrous beauty, a symphony of sound and sight in Nature's cathedral.

The words to the music are simple, but commanding in their veracity: "You must stop, look, and listen to what I have prepared for you since before you were." Here, there is no arguing, no escaping Nature's majesty. Homage cries out from within: "*Magnificat anima mea Dominum et exsultavit spiritus meus...*"7

I sit for an hour in nature's sanctuary, facing Avalanche Pass, my feet dangling from the bridge over the dam, absorbing the refreshment of the breeze sliding off the mountains, escaping down the brook,

---

5 Matthew 11:28
6 Jeremiah 31:25
7 Luke 1:46-47 "My soul proclaims the greatness of the Lord; my spirit rejoices..."

its coolness against my wet tee shirt in sharp contrast to the warmth of the sun as it reaches for Algonquin's hidden peak. To my left, Marcy, who feeds the mighty Hudson and this humble dam bearing her name, teasingly hides herself behind lesser peaks. The falls behind me, in endless prayer, chant their rhythmic mantra, allowing peace. And peace there is, and now I know.

I return the next day, like a compulsive lover, unable to say good-bye. I bring a book with me, Tony de Mello's *Awareness*, intending to spend more time at the dam. I don't.

Looking out toward Avalanche Pass, I remember the architectural splendor ahead. I wonder if I can still make it to Avalanche Lake. The compulsion now is to move on, drawn to Nature's other cathedral, sky for ceiling.

Memory reminds me of the trail (trial) that lies ahead. Is it as steep and long as I remember? Slight in comparison to Mt. Marcy and Algonquin I know, but difficult for me none-the-less. It's relative, I say, as other hikers seem to pass me effortlessly on the way.

The path is easy enough initially and then I hit the wall, the steep section about half way between the dam and the lake. I now feel I've exchanged my boots for leaden knee-highs. "Why do I do this?" That nagging question, and I wonder to myself if I really enjoy this. "One step at a time, what's the rush?" And on I go, refreshed somewhat when the trail levels out before the descent to the lake.

I am cheered on by the thin falls off the side of the mountain here, water splattering left and right. Gentle waters divided here, destined for the Atlantic, to the left as the St. Lawrence, to the right as the Hudson. This I believe is the northern most source of the Hudson River, while Lake Tear of the Clouds on the cheek of Marcy is the highest. I enjoy reflecting on this little tidbit and after a minute move on, down through the ominously narrow swampy pass, expectantly awaiting the revelation. And then, suddenly, light. I break out from the darkness of the forest into this narrow cathedral, sheer walls reaching straight to the sky, grateful for contrast. Wonder!

Lunch, rest awhile and then return. Oh, I must climb a bit again before the descent. The descent, so much easier, but I remember my fall on the way out the last time I was here. Danger is here. I'm alone and a fall could be serious. It's a long way out. I reflect on the fact that "there are no ambulances here" and have empathy for any rescuers charged with carrying me out. It wouldn't happen this night, and now I understand the importance of proper clothing, equipment, and the caution to hike in three's. Aha! Awareness.

8/29/1994

Swan and a Boy

After hiking in Fahnestock State Park I went to sit by the Hudson River. I was enjoying watching a swan swimming about ten feet a way. Along came a boy who started throwing pebbles at the swan.

"Is the swan bothering you?" I asked.

"No," the boy replied.

"Well, why are you bothering it?"

Feebly, the boy responded, "Well, in the past..."

Maybe that's why there was only one swan. I wonder how long it will last?

11/21/1994

A Child's Plea

I am a child
Fragile
Crying in a wilderness

Fear
Uncertainty and confusion
Which path to take?

Crooked or direct,
In walking
My own path I make.

Remember,
Experienced traveler,
Echoes of the past.

Your voice
The power has
To make straight my way.

Will you speak to me?

8/17/1995

Joyous Symphony

Walking in the woods:
The feel of my foot upon the ground.
Sweet smell of hemlocks.
The sound of pebbles beneath my feet,
And the gurgling of the brook.

Joyous symphony!
Each note different;
One glorious sound.
And I,
I feel like the "Hallelujah Chorus."

12/05/1996

Fools Work

The wise man knows the capacity of his
wagon.
He does not overload it,
Thus he is continually enriched.

Not knowing the capacity of his wagon,
The fool takes on more than it can carry,
Thus he is continually making repairs.

Knowing what you can carry is wisdom.
Taking on more than you can carry is fools
work.

12/16/1996

Light of Life

The child followed the Divine light within.
It led to the cross, then resurrection.

Trust the star that burns within.
It will light the way beyond the cross to life.

12/17/1996

Stars of Wonder

Look at the star in the eastern sky.

Look at the star burning within.

Stars of wonder.
Rejoice.

12/17/1996

Journey

As I set out on my hike the path is gentle and easy. Occasionally I notice the pebbles beneath my feet and now and then one gets in my boot. It irritates a bit. Sitting down, I remove it.

As I approach the mountain, the path becomes more steep and steeper yet. Pebbles morph into rocks, rocks into boulders. Huffin' and puffin', tough climb now. Only a fool would try to pull the boulders out of the way. Why do I try? They don't budge. I sit on them. Ah, that's it. Along the way we meet and walk together. I step on different rocks than you. Are you still trying to push those boulders out of the way? They're part of the path. Here, have a seat. Where does this path lead anyway? Will we arrive before nightfall?

Approaching the summit the path evens off a bit; views are spectacular. There is exhilaration now. Beyond, I see the hills and valleys previously traversed.

More suddenly than expected, darkness descends, the deep darkness found in the wilderness. Fear, panic, stranded, and alone! Terror, terror from within, brought forth by suppressed, unknown and unmet demons, rousted from a restless sleep by a vivid imagination. These demons only too willingly give life to monsters not yet met, but eagerly anticipated, monsters ready to pounce from behind every tree along the path. These phantoms inflict a cold, dry, pain, bottomless. Wrestling with them, unable to suppress them any longer, I feel the battle lost. The more I struggle the deeper the fear, the greater the panic. Exhausted by the fight, and broken by the pain, I give up.

I have wrestled with the devil and my devil has won. Another god lies shattered beneath its pedestal, the god of power and control. How many more,

23

identities as yet unknown, remain hidden within? Strange battle, this, for in the devil's conquest is my victory. I have met my devil and named it "Powerlessness."

I awake as dawn begins to break. As the sun rises dew sparkles like diamonds on wildflowers. I walk through mountain meadows, along a murmuring brook singing a soothing song. Spring waters quench my thirst. Bears are just bears now, though I'm still working on snakes. I walk around boulders on the path and feel free to wander, no longer consumed by a need to arrive at a destination. Darkness will come and so will light, new mountains and great views. And the moon at night, ah yes, the moon. When you point to it I will try not to look at your finger.

It's been a hell of a trip so far, so I think I'll just keep walking, making my own path, one step at a time. If you walk along with me great, and if you choose a different path, enjoy your hike. Watch out for the snakes.

12/25/1996

Crows Delight

Two crows
Playing on the breeze.
Cool breeze.
Watching-feeling.
Gratias.

Integrity

Thinking of you;
Thinking of me.
External commands;
External demands.
Irrelevant.

Present moment;
Precious moment.
Here I am.
This is it.
Choice.

Need not,
Want not.
Enough is enough.

Content with what I have,
Staying centered
In the present moment;
No beginning,
No end,
I can embrace myself,
Then the whole world can smile.

Commentary

I think about what it means for us to be who we are. What does it take to be complete, whole human beings? The external commands or demands of society, or individuals, belong to them. They are theirs, their urgency, not ours. It is important that we not let ourselves be yanked to and fro by them. Thus in a sense they must be irrelevant to us. Not in the sense that we don't consider them, but that we recognize that the "demand / command" part is their thing. Rather, we respond to them in the present. To the extent that they are presented to us, they are part of our reality at the only real, present moment. Consequently, we have a choice of how to be this very instant. Right here and now, everything I need is present to me, simply because that's all there is. This is it for the eternal moment. In fact, no more moments are guaranteed.

Recognizing that nothing is lacking in my participatory relationship with the creative energy of the Universe, the Universe constantly becoming, I want nothing. Fully accepting of the present reality, I am content with what I have. As long as I am able to stay with the present moment, and not lose myself in thoughts of the past or anxieties over the future, I can experience the joy, peace, and contentment, the gift of my participation in all that is, right now. In doing so, my relationship with the universal creative energy sends a ripple of joy throughout the whole Universe. The world is a happier place because I am able to trust myself right now.

I wonder if this is what St. Augustine meant by: "Love God, and do what you will"?

8/1995

JAMES CASEY

Creator Spiritus 8

What's it all about? 9
It's about dancing.
That's it!
God dancing,
The energy of the Universe,
No past; no future
Just now.
Eternal dance,
Constant Creation.

God dances,
And when God dances
There is just dance;
The Universe is.

The Universe dances
And so do we
In a cosmic singularity.
The energy of love,
Fire discovered,
Again. 10
Alpha-Omega.

11/28/1999

---

8 From the Latin hymn *Veni Creator Spiritus*, translated as "Come Creator Spirit."
9 This question is reminiscent of Joss Stone's song, "Alfie" and the movie of the same name.
10 A reference to a noted quote of Teilhard de Chardin: "Someday, after we have mastered the winds, the waves, the tides, and gravity, we will harness for God the energies of love and then, for the second time in the history of the world, humanity will have discovered fire."

Recovery Area

Today, my soul went for a walk in the forest.
A sign on a tree said: "Do not enter,
Wildlife recovery area."
Making no distinctions, I continued along,
Secure in the feeling that my soul could benefit
from the recovery.

It did.

When the mind is not disturbed by
unnecessary things,
The sounds of silence are heard,
A melody of natures wonders.
And when distraction disturbs the soul's peace
Nature's song,
Like plain chant,
Gently soothes.

12/05/1999

AΩ Alpha and Omega

Alpha 11

In principio erat Verbum. 12
The Word is spoken
A burst of creative intelligence
Manifested energy
Unfolds the Universe
A child is born
Verbum caro factum est 13
And "the world is charged
With the grandeur of God." 14

Omega 15

---

11 Alpha is the first letter of the Greek alphabet.
12 John 1:1 "In the beginning was the Word..." The original Greek word, which is translated here into Latin as *Verbum*, is *Logos*. In Greek *logos* means word, but word which has the power to effect what is spoken.
13 John 1:14 "The Word was made flesh."
14 The first line of Gerard Manley Hopkins' poem "God's Grandeur."
15 Omega is the last letter of the Greek alphabet. See Revelation 1:8; 2:8; 22:13 – Jesus, the Logos, the Word of God is the first and last, the Alpha and Omega, the beginning and the end. There is a unity here in this creation, a singularity if you will, which we can risk not seeing in our temporality. In Teilhard de Chardin's vision, the Omega Point is the point of Ultimate Unity toward which the Universe is evolving and in which individuality is preserved. The *Logos* draws all to himself. See 1 Cor 15:26-28, "that God may be all in all." These are the last words in Teilhard de Chardin's journal.

The Light of Love

Deep sorrow invades the soul
Like a thief at night in search of gold
But Memory knocking at the door,
Arouses love that warms the heart
Like dawning sun on morning dew.

Dark night vanquished
The thief retreats the amorous light
For the treasure that was sought,
Love amassed,
Cannot be filched through the portal of the
heart.

*Amor vincit omnia et nos cedamus amori.*16

---

16 "Love conquers all and let us too surrender to love" from
Virgil's Eclogues, Book X, line 69.

Prayer

Spirits, spirits everywhere
And me without a prayer
Or is it spirits, spirits nowhere
And praying friends everywhere?

To pray or not to pray
That is the question
Or to ask what is prayer
Should that be the reflection?

Questions, questions everywhere
With answers rather rare.
I search for the light
Like a child in the night
Looking for lightning bugs.

Spirit like a breath breathed
Boundless in the heavenly sky?
What need so felt
That idols we make
Of things such as these?

Yet a friend I have
Who in church he prays
For us all he says
On a scooter rides
With his wife beside
To commune with his God.

Complementarity of Opposites

Heads or tails
What difference does it make?
It's all one coin.

Is there up without down
Light without dark?
Imagine silence without sound.
What is sleep without awake?

Life and death
Two sides of the same existence.
Before distinction, what is there to realize?
Energy conserved.

Sleep or wake
Dead or alive
Or just is.
It's your choice.

Commentary

This was in response to a friend's joking question: "If you die in your sleep do you realize it in the morning when you wake up?"

12/01/1998

JAMES CASEY

On Wiseass Remarks

Those with wit so acerbic
Should not speak so quick
Lest dullness of mind
Best sharpness of tongue,
And before all mankind
Confirm how dumb.

12/04/1998

The Intelligence of the Universe

Our world,
Embedded in primordial chaos,
Unfolds.
Choices made
From day to day,
Age to age
By what intelligence unknown?

Like David,
Enshrined in a marble mountain,
Waiting.
Creative energy
Transmitted
From generation to generation
Per omnia saecula saeculorum.
What mind chooses to discard so much stone?

Commentary

Who is responsible for the magnificent creation of the statue of David? Did it come from the mind of Michelangelo, or is there a greater Mind? Could Michelangelo have created it had not the minds of others before him contributed to the creative energy of the Universe. Was Michelangelo's mind as dependent on those other minds as one brain cell is to another within the web of brain cells connected by neurotransmitters carrying the electrical energy from one cell to the next within the mind of man?

12/07/1998

Creative Energy

Each instant,
Eternal creation;
Com-union.

In the beginning was the Word 17
Et Verbum caro factum est. 18
"And the Word was made flesh."
Behold the child.

I and the Universe
No! I am the Universe,
Energy communicated,
Manifested as a
A world incarnate.

Just that!
In-car-nation. 19

7/25/1999

---

17 John 1:1. The words, "In the beginning" are the first words in
the Bible as well as the Gospel of John. See Genesis 1:1. It is no
coincidence that John begins his gospel with a creation account.
The *Logos*, the Word, effected the world and, as the next line
expresses, became of the world, com-union.
18 Latin translation of John 1:14: "And the Word was made
flesh."
19 From the Latin *Incarnationem* – the act of being made into
flesh.

Compassionate Asses AKA Agape 20

Why concern yourself
About the regard of others?
They have enough trouble
Consistently loving themselves.
Clashing cymbals!

Asses, we are all asses. 21
When you realize that,
Caring for yourself is the beginning of
wisdom.
With compassion and love,
You can embrace the world,
The Self, with passion.
Com-passion. Com-union.

Agape

---

20 *Agape*, the Greek word for love. In the Christian community a
fraternal spiritual love, deep respect and affirmation of the other
as distinct from *Eros*. In the original Greek, it is the last word of
chapter 13 of 1 Corinthians.
21 The late Anthony De Mello, S.J., in his book *Awareness*, says
he wants to write a book entitled "I'm an Ass, You're an Ass." It
is a takeoff of Thomas Harris' book, *I'm OK—You're OK*.

Just Us

The master knows
He participates in creative energy.
And everything that is
Is energy.

Therefore he cares for things,
Just as a skilled artist
Cares for his brushes.

He knows that everything that is
Is sacred creation,
An manifestation of Self.

The Learned Man

The truly learned man
Knows the time for talk,
And the time for silence,
The time for scholarly study,
And the time to watch a rose.

He knows why the turtle prefers
To drag its tail in the mud,
Rather than be enshrined on an altar. 22

---

22 The reference here to "the turtle" is from: Merton, Thomas. "The Turtle." *The Way Of Chuang Tzu*. New York: New Directions, 1969. 93–94. Print.

Peace

Many fail to find peace.
Contentment eludes them.
The search an endless pursuit;
The prize beyond reach.

Expectations of what should be,
Unwilling to accept the way things are,
Driven to control the world.
No wonder.

No wonder at all.

Harmony

To know well or to live well,
which is better?
With perfection,
there is imperfection.
Before wisdom,
there is a dark night of the soul.
Before awareness,
silence.
Better to listen to the sounds of the forest
than the dialogues of scholars.
Better self-knowledge
than knowledge of the Universe.
Or are they the same?
To live in harmony
with the way things are,
this is best of all.

Silence, the Gateway to Self-Knowledge

Idle chatter is the friend of superficiality.
Incessant noise nurtures a clouded mind.
A clouded mind encourages self-delusion.
Delusion feeds on greed and
self-aggrandizement.
Greed and self-aggrandizement,
the stuff of scandal and corruption.
What's the use of that?

Let go of unnecessary talk.
Avoid useless noise.
Risk the silence.
Silence, the gateway to self-knowledge.
Mindfulness, the path to peace.
When you are at peace,
There is peace in the world.
Does that make sense?

Gift to the World

In the end, who cares
how many books you have read,
how many speeches you have made?
But to walk with you quietly in the forest,
what a joy!
A gift to the world.
A memory forever.
Energy rippling through the Universe.
It cannot be stopped.

Non-attachment to the Wisdom of Others

The Enlightened One is open to what is.
He makes his path by walking in the present.
The blind man is caught in the past or future.
He seeks to follow the path of others.
Thus he stubs his toe.

Enlightenment is not following the master's
path.
It is in following the master's way.
The master trusts the light within.
In the present moment, he makes his path,
one step at a time.
Trusting the light within, the blind man sees.
In the present, he can make his path, one step
at a time.
Thus enlightened, he finds his own way.
The master's way.

The Enlightened One is not attached to
authority.
"Trust the light within."
This is the teaching of the master.
It is superior to all other teachings.
Why then attach yourself to the teachings of
experts?
Experts upon experts!
Where does it stop?

The superior man knows,
There is no superior man.

11/27/1998

A Mighty Mountain

Turning, turning, turning,
Turning wheel
Cycling life
Throughout the night,
Life upon life
And the 33 rise up, 23

Emerging to the light,
Plato's prisoner from the cave,
Lazarus from the tomb,
Jonah from the whale,
And Noah from the ark,
To life renewed.

Out of the depths
They cried to thee O Lord (see Psalm 130)
And you brought them up from Sheol
To stand before a fractured world
Like a mighty mountain, (see Psalm 30)
Solid in solidarity,

A resurrection and ascension
Witnessed by a world
In need of healing.

In celebration of goodness,
Humanity rejoices
At a reflection of its solid self
Mirrored in the heart of the 33
And the spirit of the steadfast.

---

23 On August 5, 2010, thirty-three miners were trapped when the
San José Mine in the Atacama Desert in Chile caved-in. After 69
days, on October 13, 2010, the men, 2,300 feet underground, were
raised to the surface in a capsule one at a time.

45

Earth, once molten rock
From which life emerged,
Through solid rock
Gave birth again
And clothed its own
With wisdom, character,
And grace for new life,
Testimony to the doubting,
Hope for humanity that
Salvation in solidarity lies.

Sartre repudiated.
L'enfer, ce n'est pas les autres. 24
Hell is not other people.
Within the hand of man,
The key to paradise lies.

---

24 In one of the last lines of his play, *No Exit* (*Huis Clos*, in French), Jean-Paul Sartre has his character, Garcin, say, "Hell is other people" (In French, "*L'enfer, c'est les autres.*")

Reflection on An Evening Prayer

An Evening Prayer offered
Like a silent hand
Reaching across mountains,
Down through valleys,
Over waters turbulent and placid,
Distance defied,
To touch a heart gently.

Could this be the hand of God
Who in silence speaks
The thought gift of a friend
That soothes the soul
To sleep in peace
Beneath the same Moon
That overhead is beaming?

A Christmas Thought

For John Richard Hannaway

With the birth of a child
Light bursts forth into the world
And Creation flows
Incarnating the earth
With Sacred life
For eyes to see
To warm hearts
To creative work
For a blessed future.

Light illuminates darkness,
Energy of love,
Spark of hope,
Ignites a wonderful Creation.
"Dixitque Deus fiat lux
Et facta est lux."[25]
And in his hand Man discovers fire.

---

25 Genesis 1:3 "And God said, 'Let there be light,' and there was light."

Spring

Gently touched by Nature's warmth
The flower rising up unfolds.
Stamens stiffen.
Spring aroused
Bursts forth in a majesty of color
And we have eyes to see.
And we feel Nature's breath
Bathe us in perfumes
Subtle and soft.
Its pollen births the joy of life.

I hear a crow calling.
Just beautiful!

JAMES CASEY

Summer

Beneath the stars I lie
Gazing out in wonder,
In delight, to share
The majesty and mystery
Of Deneb, Vega, and Altair
With a friend afar who dares
Search the same twinkling lights,
Sky of shimmering sights,
For The Summer Triangle
Beaming in celestial blackness,
Within which The Swan and Eagle
Soar to the sweet vibrations of The Lyre.

Via Dolorosa

Right now, today,
The World is walking,
Walking the *Via Dolorosa*
Toward Golgotha.
Awhile back, years ago,
Love walked,

Walked the Sorrowful Road
To death on Calvary
That we might know
That love is the way,
Agape love,
The way to salvation.

Now, this very day,
The World is on fire
As it marches,
Marches with a sickness,
To death,
Along the *Via Dolorosa*.

Who lit the torch,
Set the World ablaze?
Who is responsible?
Do I have a hand on the match,
The match that lit the torch
That set the World on fire?

Where lies the road,
The road to salvation?
Who dares to walk it?
Do we have eyes to see,
To see the future,
The future of our World?

JAMES CASEY

Like the match
That lit the torch
That set the World ablaze,
The future is in our hands.

Love, the energy of love,
Can it yet spark,
Spark a conflagration
To consume the fire of death?

Will we walk the road to salvation,
The way of agape love to life
Or will we take the road to Calvary,
The way to death , extinction?

The World is in our hands
"We must love one another or die." 26

---

26 From the movie, "tuesdays with morrie," Executive Producers, Oprah Winfrey and Kate Forte. The film is based on the book by Mitch Albom, written for television by Tom Rickman. The quote is originally from the W.H. Auden poem, "September 1, 1939."

Love's Embrace

Love has no body,
But like light,
In silence,
Warms the heart,
Penetrates the darkness.

It illuminates what is,
Touches the soul,
Radiating from the lover
Like the sun's gift
Birthing life.

Love's embrace
Extinguishes the divide.
There is no lover
Just the loved.
A flame burns within,

Eternal energy of life.
With the eyes of the soul
Silently one beholds
An affirmation of goodness,
The nativity of beauty.

With fire in the heart
The face of the world
Is changed forever
That which has no body
An eternal incarnation.

12/9/2012
11:00 am

JAMES CASEY

The Candle of the Innocents

On that day
That day of wrath
Evil incarnate came to town
Came to Newtown, Connecticut
To exercise the insanity of Adam 27
In the slaughter of the Innocents

Each one a gift to the World
A twinkling star
The light of pure joy
That Lucifer wanted to reclaim
On that day
That day of madness that day of shame

Snuffing out the candle of life
Leaving darkness
The darkness of the night
The long dark night of the soul
The Long dark night

Out of the depths of darkness we cry
We cry for a why for a why
For a why that will never satisfy
Yet starlight burns still
In heaven above

In hearts below
Today an incarnation of grief
Agony beyond belief
Yet an eternal flame
Will lighten with pure joy
The hearts of the living
For burns within the candle of the Innocent

---

27 Adam was the name of the killer. Ironically, it is also the name
of the first man in Genesis. The word Adam means man.

54

On this day
This day of recollection
Day of the Sun
God's day
Some will ask
Demand like Job perhaps
Of Him the reason why

In the prevailing silence
Can we ponder perchance
Beyond projection onto God
Reasons or lack thereof
And plumb the depths
The depths of our own souls

And ask what sin lies within
What sickness prevails in the land
For since Adam's sin
We have been here awhile

Evolving all along as this Universe
Earth from stars made
And us of this same stuff emerge
To sing the praises of a God on high
And create the world of tomorrow
For this ongoing creation
Is in our hands now
A gift of God to Adam
Who taking earth into His hands
Made Man in His own image
In His likeness He made him

Homo Sapiens we call ourselves
Homo Creator we are
Sapiens not yet

JAMES CASEY

This is our work now
God gave us the key to Heaven
The same key opens the gates of Hell
When will we have the wisdom
The wisdom to open the celestial gates
That is the question
Not why but when
When will we ever learn

Lucifer snuffed out life
But the light he could not claim

12/16/2012
12:34pm

Eternal Are The Ghosts

Beautiful and warm
Eternal are those ghosts
Written in your heart
They have taken up residence
A long time now
Stroll they the pathways
Sail the synapses of your mind
Through stormy seas and placid waters
Bringing joy to your dreams
Your flesh is their flesh now

You a universe of sorts
Peopled with living spirits
Like stars radiating warmth and light
Limitless energy unfolding memories
Passed from age to age
Ideas igniting an incarnation
An eternal nativity of familial spirits
And you thought you were just you

A gift to the world
Like the light of the sun
Seen through the mist
A rainbow of colors
Delighting and enlightening
Brightening dare I say
Pilgrims along the way
Whose stories will be told
Written memories in souls
Souls yet to unfold
Per omnia saecula saeculorum
Forever and ever

JAMES CASEY

Light

Lux fulgebit hodie super nos 28
As it does every day
Light illumines the world
And our own private world as well
With brightness that beautifies beauty itself

Yet sometimes
Like the swift strike of lightning
The sharp clap of thunder
Ringtone intrusion shatters
Routine serenity of everyday matters

Unexpectedly and unwelcomed
Darkness surges over that land
Rolling thick turbulent storm clouds
Rapidly below the radiant crystal
Clear sharpness of the day
Then hanging like a dense weight
On the shoulders of the world

A stomach faints away
Leaving empty despair
A dark hollow gut
Forlorn ever to be filled again
A heart has collapsed
Sunk below the depths
To the frigid waters
Beyond the golden rays of sunlight
Believing that it shall never rise
Again to be embraced in warmth
It is the death of joy

---

28 "Light burst forth upon us today," referring to the birth of Jesus in the Roman Catholic liturgy from the *Introit* of the Mass at Dawn on Christmas day.

A shadow envelops our world
Inflicting a dull melancholic atmosphere
Deeper than dreadful darkness
Deeper than the dead of night
And as the Psalmist in despair prays
"Out of the depth we cry to thee O Lord
Lord hear our prayer"
So too do we have hope
Like the watchman longing
For the dawn of the new day 29

Light does follow darkness as day the night
Storm clouds weep over the land
Emptying their grief for verdant life to grow
Radiance too bursts through darkness
A revelation that brighter days can bestow
A resurrection of warmth
Cultivate compassion
Curry courage
To take up the light of life again

So I stand and watch clouds come and go
The sun too passes through the sky
From dawn to dusk and then the night
I watch the eternal flow of grief and joy
They too pass through me
Just I remain
Like the sky I do not grasp
Knowing this too shall pass
For night cannot detain day
Nor darkness constrain the light

---

29 Reference to psalm 130 in the Hebrew numbering system, 129
in the Septuagint.

Looking for Truth

As I walked through life
Along flourishing paths
And wearisome ways
Through verdant vales,
Desolate dales,
Blessed blue skies above,
Ominous storm clouds low,
Dark in a rolling roiling firmament,
I remember my dreams
Of days of innocence,
Institutions of integrity
Supporting a sunny world,
Solid in solidarity.

I believed in those days.
I believed in the veracity of man
And his truthful ways,
Of bankers, lawyers, politicians, and priests,
Popes and presidents too.
I believed in God, the Deity,
And trusted the corporate entity.
As I wander I wonder,
Did I make an idol of Truth
In a land of naiveté
As I prayed to God in Heaven above?

Today,
As I tread along the way,
I create my own path
Through choices I make day by day.
I see a fractured world,
A shattered world,
Suffering sadly through a lack of veracity.

Truth,
Has it been sacrificed to a god of immorality
On an altar of expediency and commerciality?
Or has the beacon of light
That once saved forlorn sailors
From losing their site
Been abandoned to the night
By keepers of the light?

As I wander now, I wonder,
I wonder where truth has gone
And how the world,
Sailing in the barque of humanity,
Will sail the stormy seas
And settle on the shores of serenity.

7/2/2013
11:03 pm

Heaven

My friend dreams
Dreams of his parents
In the heavenly estate
Warm memories has he
Of drinking tea together
Around the kitchen table

He creates poems about it
And shares them with me
Not me alone of course
But like a child skipping a rock
On placid waters
He sends out waves of joy

Ideas of love and union
Com-union really
He and his parents are one
Ripples of energy without end
An example of it am I
Sitting here writing a poem

And he wonders my friend
Wonders about that heavenly place
They tell him that God is love
He has no time for recriminations
There is no hell
Even Hitler is in that heavenly place
Hard to imagine of course

In my dreams
I dream the God of love
We walk through the Valley of Death
And He tells me He has no time for hell
The God of love has no time for hell
For Man has created that place quite well
Without any help from me says He

Look how they torture themselves
And then one another eternally

In my dreams I ask
The God of love I ask
What makes this place heavenly
Look over there says He
See Socrates arguing with Ulysses
Who is itching to set sail with his mariners
Both pursuing knowledge
Like stars beyond the horizon
A joyful journey of endless dialog

And the Deity said to me
See there the parent's of your friend
Sipping tea at the kitchen table in serenity
They are all aglow in celestial harmony
That tea alone is heavenly
Tell Dennis said He
That glow you see in your dream
Is the refulgent radiance of you
For Florrie and Johnny are one with you
The three of you in unity
That is what makes this place so heavenly
The three of you form one reality
A trinity of solidarity

Ordinary Things

I look out my bedroom window
Ordinary things I see
Leaves gently fluttering
A dappled green world calm and true
Silent as a summer breeze
Silence seducing sleep so secure
Suggesting slumber in serenity
You would think the world is at peace

Not so in the land of Pharaoh
Where intolerance without cease
Preys in the name of Allah so
Like a beast cannibalizing
It devours its own in the street
In the name of God it does this
How explain this insanity
A world without humanity

In the name of God how explain
A world lacking in harmony
A world without humanity

Insanity

I look out my bedroom window
Ordinary things do I see
Pray a world of serenity

8/16/2013
7:17 pm

A Thought at Christmas

With the birth of a child
Light is incarnated
Given flesh that is
A gift to the world
It burst forth upon us this day 30
And creation flows
Forward with a force
A force forever fluent
To speak truth to darkness

But this birthed world
Still in darkness lies
Lies told by men to men
While children with eyes
Eyes of wonder
Wonder
How a world can survive
When truth has become
A stranger in a stranger land

This world cries out in pain
As men unworthy of the name
Seek self in power and fame
As if blinded by the darkness
That in their hearts they claim
For they have wrung the light of truth
From the ventricles of life
As they trod the trail of Lucifer
Down the days and nights

---

30 From the Second Mass At Dawn, December 25, The Nativity of Our Lord. "A light shall shine upon us this day." See also Isaiah 9:2 "The people that walked in darkness, have seen a great light: to them that dwelt in the region of the shadow of death, light is risen."

With time to slaughter one another
As if the other were not their brother
And do it in the name of God
The same whom they claim
To be their creator
This God who in silence speaks
Through beauty harmony and mystery
And leaves us guessing through catastrophe
Can this God be seen in the eyes of the other

By going out of ourselves to our brother
Forgetting self as we trod the trail of life
Lighting the way with the torch of integrity
Pursuing truth wherever it may lead
Creating the day with openness and harmony
Knowing that the world of tomorrow
Depends on our refulgence today
For we were born light incarnated
A gift to the world for all to see

12/17/2013
10:25 pm

The God Idea

The idea of god
It is man made
The idea that is
It is not god
The word man
That is not man
It has not flesh
No blood either
It points to an idea
An idea we have
Of flesh and blood
Mind too and more
A meme *sans* genes

What is this man
Man without woman
An idea in some distress
Imagine no horse
No hippo either
Man but no lion
Not even a tigress
And this god
Without man
Imagine that
How imagine this god
A god without man
Can you imagine that

12/25/2013
1:15 pm

Heart of Love

A poem for Charlie Giglio on being named semi-finalist as Teacher of the Year.

Thank God for the sun
Earth is warmed
Flowers bloom
Fruits flourish
Charlie's heart burns with a glow
Spread in a garden of love
Fertile soil from which children sprout
With minds and hearts aglow
In full flower will disseminate seeds
Seeds of *caritas et amor* 31
Sol's bountiful radiance
For a world at night in need of light
Exsultemus, et in ipso jucundemur 32
Let us rejoice and be pleased in him.

5/11/2014
2:00 PM

---

31 Latin phrase, *caritas et amor* from the Christian hymn, "*Ubi Caritas et Amor.*" *Caritas* means charity, the spiritual love that affirms the other and holds the other in deep respect, and *amor*, with affectionate love."
32 Latin phrase "*Exsultemus, et in ipso jucundemur*" from the Christian hymn, "*Ubi Caritas et Amor,*" means "Let us rejoice and be pleased in him." Charles Giglio subsequently became the 2015 New York State Teacher of the Year.

A Jewel of a Story

I have a story
Written in my mind.
I hold it in memory
As if inscribed in stone.
I want to see it as it was,
Ignore the flow of time,
As if to acknowledge change
Would eliminate a treasured jewel.

I know the work of time
From budding leaf in lush spring
To golden autumn's desiccated fall
Before winter snow obliterates all
In pure angelic white,
Frozen,
An eternal blanket over all.

Yet I hold to an image old,
Not in explicit memory,
Definite in line and form,
More nebulous than that,
Infused with feeling,
A warm fire in the hearth
On a cold and frigid day,
Soft and playful as a puppy.

A smile I see, innocent with life.
It's music plays in my mind
Like Mozart's Piano Concerto Number 21,
Elvira Madigan - just as lovingly.

10/08/2014
11:55 AM

The Path to Peace

This is the way it is
Just this
Right now
Nothing lacking

Yet between heaven and hell
Through will, want, and desire
I attach to a world of expectations
And place this self in Dante's ring of fire

He is not to blame though
Dante painted in words wise
While I created with mental desire
A cage to enslave my soul born free
Locked with imagined chains
Of the way things should be

Imagine if I imagine
There is no way things should be
My soul could flee
The cage of desire
The self made ring of fire

"Learn to love the confusion"
A friend spoke to my heart
I did not understand then
Now I know the path to peace
This is just the way it is
        And
Sometimes the lion eats the lamb

10/14/2014
Revised
2/25/2016

From the Stars to the Stars

In our hands salvation lies.
Praying Jesus passes the buck.
He pointed the way for us to see.
"Ubi caritas et amor Deus ibi est," 33
Where there is profound respect
And deep affection, there is God.
What more do we need to be,
To be in peace upon this earth?

I bow to the divinity in you,
In all of us,
Fire that fuses starlight into creative energy
Forging a brighter world
From chaos to cosmos.

Radiant light burst forth
On the day that you were born.
A bright supernova infusing darkness,
Encounters the satanic in us all.
And the struggle for integrity unfolds
As the soul journeys that long road
Where unwelcome night invades the day.

Darkness overcomes a sun filled day.
Yet starlight is a sign of hope
For a resurrection of the sun.
With faith in that we know:
Sun's energy warms our hearts,
Burns in our bones as well,
A cosmic unity the Universe gifts itself,
Risks itself with us,
For some will extinguish the light,

---

33 See note 31. The phrase translates: "Where there is charity and love, there is God" or another, "Where there is profound respect and deep affection, there is God."

Invite the spirit of darkness,
Ride with the posse of death and destruction.

That torch of creation,
An eternal inheritance,
Passed from generation to generation.
Is in our hands now.

We, *Homo Creator*,
Energy of the sun,
Very stuff of suns,
Suns upon suns.

Sacrifice of dying stars
Transforms death to life,
"Star stuff" as incarnated imagination,
Life, the light of the world.

Knowing that, we can ride,
Ride with the angels of life.
Through the valley of death we can ride
Illuminating the dawn with the fire of love.

Et lux in tenebris lucet.
"and light shines in the darkness" 34
Darkness will not abide it.
Love forging the world of tomorrow.
Sic itur ad astra. 35
"This is the way to the stars."

12/8/2014
6:17 PM

---

34 *Et lux in tenebris lucet* is Latin for "and light shines in the darkness," Jn1:5
35 *Sic itur ad astra* is the original Latin from The *Aeneid* book IX, line 641, an epic Latin poem by Virgil. It translates as: "This is the way to the stars."

Shining Stars

Those that teach
With hearts on fire
Justice and virtue
Are the Star of Bethlehem
A guiding light to truth
A sign of faith
To those in darkness

Daniel said it 36
De La Salle too 37
They shall shine
Shine as stars
For all eternity

Among shining stars
Of stellar students
They shall shine
A galactic gathering
Constellation of stars
Rejoicing in celestial light
And together singing
Honneur à Toi
Glorieux De La Salle 38

11/23/2015
2:40 pm

---

36 Dn 12:3

37 **Meditations** by John Baptist de La Salle, edited by Augustine Loes, FSC and Francis Huether, FSC. Lasallian Publications, 1994, reprinted 2007. P 471, meditation 208.2.

38 *Honneur à Toi Glorieux De La Salle* is the title of a French hymn honoring St. John Baptist de La Salle, founder of the religious order, Brothers of the Christian Schools. The translation is: Honnor to you Glorious De La Salle.

A World Illuminated
A Christmas Thought Again

Lux fulgebit hodie super nos 39

A child is born
And with this life
Light burst forth
The world is illuminated
"That they may have life
And have it to the fullest" 40

Each child a gift to the world
A supernova of creative energy
Born with the key
To open the gates of Paradise
Paradise now if only we would see
We get to choose the way to be

Each photon an elementary particle
Yet radiating together
Darkness they obliterate
A refulgent world they create
A beatific vision where all can see
The truth about what it means to be

1/1/2016
1:17 pm

---

39 See note 28
40 Jn 10:10

That

Enough of that!
That is here to stay.
For even a president
Was known to say,
"That woman."
And I bet you know
That woman
And in what context too
That president denied
That he wanted to sow
Sow in her the seed of life.

So, THAT has life.
That phrase will live,
Live in infamy
That will.
That will pierce the ear
As long as someone
Is there or here to hear.
So, take THAT!

Is THAT really enough?

That is here to stay,
For there is no way
For anyone to say
That
Without THAT.
So, that is THAT.
That is all there is to that.
That may not ring bells
But try to get along
Without THAT.

Enough!
I really wanted to say
Only an egg is *un oeuf*
But enough of that.

OMG, there again is That.
Is there no end to that?
Now THAT is enough
While an egg is *un oeuf*.
Enough is enough!

1/12/2016
8:47 am

A Walk in Amity Forest

On the Eve of Surgery
My friend tells me to walk in the forest
Leave my anxieties among the trees
They will be whispering support for me

Grateful for poetic imagination
I approach the forest edge
Shades of grey suggest winter
Sunshine warms my face
My heart as well
Cold days are on the wane

I see beyond the grey a hint of red
Red budding through brown buds
Buds yearning to burst in days ahead
The force of life reaching for the sun
Sunshine eager to sacrifice itself
Urging a vibrant verdant vision of life

Each tree a friend radiating the sun's energy
Gifting itself to me
Like sunshine upon my face
Friends brighten my day
I let myself feel the warmth
The same sun that energizes the trees
Energizes me
And together we get to be
A forest of supportive amity

Walking among the trees I hear the whisper
My spirit is magnified with gratitude
My soul rejoices
Resounds with Bach's "*Magnificat*"
Oh what an "Ode to Joy"

2/28/2016

77

Gratitude

Ah! To see
To see my world green up
Day to day I watch
The forest thicken
Till the mountain fades
Behind a dappled green curtain
Wrought from April's sun
Spilling warmth on earth
Each tree reaches out
To grasp the gift of life

Ah! To feel
I too reach out
Luxuriating in the light
To grasp the gift
The sun bestows
Joyful in the warmth to know
To know that I know
That I see
That I feel
I feel this wonderful warmth

I reflect on my gratitude
For the energy of the sun revealed
That I am the energy of the sun
Revealed

4/23/2016
2:35 pm

A Paradise Mind

Digging in the dirt
Close to my roots I get
There is peace in that dirt
A paradise sort of mind
As I dig in it
Feel it
Smell it
Plant in it
An optimistic sort of mind

Then of course
The dirt reminds me
A return to the source
Will come one day
And I will rest in it
Planted eternally

From the earth
I came
Of the earth
I am
To the earth
I will return

And new life will rise
"Of the earth, earthy"[41]

4/24/2016
10:32 am

---

41 See 1 Corinthians 15:47

The Sounds of Silence

Before all, Silence is,
Sound from which
All sound sets out,
The sound of silence
Before the bang,
The Big Bang that is.
Origin of The Origin
From which creativity flows,
Primordial silence,
Origin of all possibilities.

Silence is a diamond.
Its facets sparkle
A rainbow of truth,
For truth is found
In the silence of the forest,
In watching the river flow
As it carves a mountain,
Hard rock surrendering
To water's soft touch.

Not just truth though,
Silence speaks love
With a touch
Where hollow words fail.
Wisdom knows the difference.
Peace is found there too,
Found where silence abides,
A place self can discover Self.

Perhaps absence of noise
Is silence that I seek,
Desire to escape cacophony,
Human hullabaloo,
Designed distraction,
Not absence of all sound,

Not pure silence,
For leaves rustle in the forest
And the gurgling of the mountain brook,
Nature's mantra,
Provides peaceful silence.
Sweeps away preoccupations,
A cleansing of the mind,
So I can be here not there,
To rest in the moment,
Hear the sounds of silence,
Sophia's silent whisper.

6/14/2016

The Robin Visits

The robin visits each day
Stays awhile perched on the deck rail
Cocks its head
Looks here and there
Up and down
Seems to survey its world

A gentle breeze
Leaves in the trees
Flicker sun and shadow
I wonder while I watch
What the robin wonders while it watches
Is it distracted by unnecessary things

Or is it just here enjoying the moment
As I am with gratitude
Gratitude for being here and not there
Lost in silence
Reflecting on a robin
Reflecting in silence

6/14/2016
11:27 am

In Silence Watching

Sitting in silence
Silent words only
Work my mind
Watching leaves flutter
Puffs of clouds pass
The sky is blue
Silent words fail
Feelings pervade

Another puff invades
Floats slowly by
Just blue now
Surrounded by dappled green
Fluttering gently in the soft breeze
Would that all the world could be
Just here now
Watching silently

Peace there would be

8/28/2016
11:00 am

Wonder at Wondering

Rain down dew ye heavens from above
Let the earth open and bud forth 42 life
Miracle of miracles
An invisible chain of warmth
Binding earth to sun
Animates atoms to Adam
Molten rock to consciousness

Here I stand
Among individuals apart
Of the same stuff made
Star stuff
Earth stuff
Light of light

From chaos to cosmos
A Universe of unity
Of the earth earthy
Energy of the sun
Flows through my heart
Animates my consciousness
I wonder at wondering

I wonder about life
Wonder about death
I see stars in the night sky
Wonder if they are still there
Wonder if they have died long ago
Giving life to new suns
Life to us

---

42 See Isaiah 45:8 from which the line is adapted. There are many different translations depending on the particular version of the Bible. I have added the word life in place of "savior" or "salvation."

I wonder at wondering
The consciousness of the Universe
A unity of individuals
Bound by the chain of being
Separateness an illusion
Wondering about the flow
Of the Universe of unity

2/7/2017
11:21 am

JAMES CASEY

Sophia

The world is a mysterious place.
We like to think we know
We have seen the tree of knowledge,
But a green leaf or two
Does not even a sapling make.
Is this a self-inflicted deceit?
What does the world hold like a black ace
In clutched hand from our conceit?
A dark matter indeed with energy replete.

We strive to reach beyond the curtain
To see the truth complete.
Well not everyone,
Truth for some is inconvenient,
A convenient myth a path preferred.
Does God in wisdom hold the cards,
Reveal just a bit here and there?
Perhaps we fabricate this idea of God
To soothe our knowledge incomplete
Of a world beyond our reach.

Yet scientists have faith
In a Universe complete.
It follows laws so neat.
They trust in order,
Unity a hope so sweet.
They seek an equation,
A formula so to speak;
A theory so complete
It explains everything.

But the question remains:
Is there a who who lit the torch,
Who put the fire in the equations,
A creative conflagration
Fusing elements with consciousness,

Hearts with *agape* love
To forge in the furnace of life
A Universe of wholeness,
A world that sings
Mahler's sacred symphony? 43
Each note apart
Yet united with voices
Vibrates a world in harmony,
Redeemed by energies of love.
Veni Creator Spiritus! 44

But when you come,
Creator Spirit,
Come not alone.
Let the breath of Sophia
Along with thee
Inspire our souls with humility
Like the knowledge of Socrates,
So that we may create with wisdom
The world of tomorrow.

1:30 pm
3/7/2017

---

43 Mahler's Symphony No. 8, sometimes referred to as The Symphony of 1,000 Voices, is in two parts united by the common theme of redemption through love.
44 *Veni Creator Spiritus*, translated as "Come Creator Spirit" is the Latin hymn for Pentecost. It is Part I of Mahler's Symphony No. 8.

De Colores A Song I Sing

I'm with ya, man,
I don't want to quit now either.
Rather than death I prefer to be.
Let the light of life inspire me.
Even with silence I like that light.
Silence a gift of aging to me
As long as colors I can see.

Grateful I learned it long ago,
Le Grand Silence,
In our *Grande Chartreuse.*
Memories of walking meditation
Mornings (at 5:15) under starry sky
Clear crisp air, winter's frigid stillness
Waking a sleepy monk
To see through darkness the dawn of light.

Right now in silence, bright snow I see
Like transcendent brilliance blinding me.
White silhouetted against a mountain
Gray expecting ruddy buds
On the cusp of colorful spring.
Tomorrow the Marching of the Green.

Sun piercing clouds backed by azure blue,
Edges so sharp and shining bright
I cannot look. It hurts my sight,
But grateful am I to still pursue
With Ulysses and his mariners
Knowledge like a sinking star
Beyond the horizon of darkness
To the light of a new dawn forever true.

Not yet, Dark Knight,
Though alongside you stride.
Not yet, silent darkness of eternal night.
I still have a song to sing
Before the silence of that dark night,
De Colores as of yore
"*Y por eso los grandes amores*
De muchos colores me gustan a mí." 45

11:39 am
3/16/2017

---

45 *De Colores* is a Spanish language folk song used in the Roman Catholic Cursillo movement. The title can be translated into English as "Many Colors." The translation of "*Y por eso los grandes amores / De muchos colores me gustan a mí*" is: "And for this reason the great love of many colors brings pleasure to me."

JAMES CASEY

Celebrating a Life

For Kristin

> The trees were budding up
> Earth was anxiously awaiting
> New life to color the land
> Forsythia hinting at yellow
> When the light of life burst
> Into our world for the second time
> Angels announcing God's cosmic gift
> Singing joy to the world
> I felt it in my heart
>
> The sun penetrating earth
> Warms perennial plants
> To bring forth new life
> Fragrant flowers fill fields
> Radiant colors abound
> Hummingbirds flutter about
> As do bees and butterflies
> While cardinals sing songs
> Sounds of joy celebrating the day
> Everyday like the day you were born
>
> I feel it still in my heart
> Choirs of angels
> Singing joy to the world
> Because your loving spirit
> Permeates my life
> Like the fragrance of lilac
> On a warm spring day

The world too is a better place
Filled with radiant color and fragrance
Fields of sunflowers lavender and phlox
Like Kuroki's garden in spring
You are a gift of love and life

4/9/2017
2:29 pm
Revised
7/23/2017
12:32 pm

A Numinous Web

I see things
Individual objects
People trees the sky above
Stars at night the moon I love

Apart from one another
Stars seem to float in space
From whence did they come
And where do they go

Dark emptiness between
Stable space it seems
What does it mean
Was it always there

Without emptiness
Where would we be
Without us
What would it be

Emptiness the gift of separateness
Which is easy for us to see
We don't have to ask
Is that all there is to reality

Reality is not what it seems
Superficiality masks a deeper stream
Awareness too easily abandoned
To comfort of coherent worldviews

Instead a numinous web weaves
A wondrous world out of sight
Of plasma atoms and elements of might
Mites march in time the evolutionary highway

Threads of the cosmic web unite
A Universe of unity a grand reality
Cosmological beings of cosmic stuff
A thread with consciousness

Here we be
Wondering about reality
The world we see
And the one we don't

July 17, 2017
7:15 pm

Kuroki's Garden

A story touches my heart
Of a wife who cannot see
Living in a world most dark
Gone blind rather rapidly

A husband with concern deep
For a wife so sweet but sad
Searches solutions to keep
Her from going totally mad

He has a small garden sweet
Of pink phlox fragrant in bloom
And digs in the dirt for neat
Blossoms to slay the gloom

With fragrance to entice
His lonely wife outdoors
To sit in the garden so nice
Pink flowers all over the floor

Visitors it will invite
With the sweet smell and the sight
To keep her company just right
And fill her dark life with great light

Mr. Kuroki's love story
Garden of love gift of life
To those trapped in darkness
"Love conquers all
Let us give ourselves to love!" 46

7/27/2017
4:15 pm

---

46 From Virgil's Eclogues X.69

Poetic Experience

A creative pulse I feel
The pleasure of a poem
It says write your experience
What touches you

The world grabs my innards
And twists
Aware am I of suffering and sorrow
Shattered lives of children sitting in scree

Tear scarred faces staring blankly
Staring straight out at me
While siblings scrabble debris
Searching for parents buried beneath
Skeletons of bombed out buildings
Once shelters of safety and serenity

Half a world away
In the land of rich and plenty
Children see parents stressed
Suffering a lack of serenity
The sense of safety and security
Stockholders share shuns them

While elites in power
Who have nothing to fear
Quibble over who should share
The growing cost of medical care

8/3/2017
6:15 pm

JAMES CASEY

My Grandson By My Side

With gratitude to James

Today my grandson by my side
We watched the river go by
The mighty Hudson River flow by
According to Mohican lore
The "river that flows both ways"

We talked about the river
The highest source
The glacial tarn that sits
Like a tear in the clouds
High on Marcy's shoulder

And when this mountain lake
Lake Tear of the Clouds weeps
The soft overcomes the hard
Soft soft water hard rock erodes

Sweet tears a mountain shreds
As a river cuts through it
Cuts through the Hudson Highlands
On its way to the sea

My grandson and I could see it
As we stood looking north
Through the Gate of the Highlands
From the Village of Cold Spring
On the shore of this mighty fjord

We watched this river flow both ways
As fresh water from tributaries north
Met up with salt water from the sea
He asked me then about salinity
Wanting to know how salt
Got into ocean water

A good question I told him
Proud of him for thinking
What I never thought before
Together we Googled it
To see what we could see

And now we understand
What flows out to the sea
Water washes minerals
That we can taste
But cannot see
Dissolved from rock
Sodium and more

What a joy
To learn something new
My grandson by my side

8/3/2017
6:15 pm

Love

Love, romantic love, euphoric ecstasy,
The high that seems to enliven earth itself,
Even the stars sparkle, the moon shines above.
I float amongst bright brilliant stars.
With desire complete,
It seems.
No wonder love conquers all,
It seems.
What more could I want?
This is it!
It seems.
For the moment,
This is it.

For the moment,
This love seems about me
More than you,
But of course I love you too,
That's what I say.
I love you
For what you do to me,
For what you do for me.
You make my world complete.
Complete me is what you do.

Or so I feel.
You too, no doubt?
I do. I feel so, also.
We are in love, no?
We are in love, so.

Like Narcissus loving his reflection
And discovering emptiness,
Two selves with a hole for a soul
Search for completeness.

Like the question to Alfie
We are asked by Life itself
What's it all about,
Is it just for the moment we live? 47

We do live for the moment,
For the moment is all there is.
It is always the moment that is.
An eternal now we live.

In the moment death or life resides.
Like a bird freed from the cage,
I can choose to soar high above
Or look for the nearest farm
To hang with turkeys down below.

The key to the cage is in my hands.
I can open the prison gate of my mind,
Unlock the cultural chains I let bind
And free the slave within.
I get to choose to be all that I can be.

I believe in love, Alfie
Without true love we just exist, Alfie,
As if to breathe were life itself.
But Life reached out to me and said:
No one else can make you whole.
Life provides you the capacity to love.
You were born a gift to the world
The gift you give the other makes you whole.

8/11/2017
12:26 am

---

47 *Alfie* is a 1966 film, adapted by William Naughton from his play and novel of the same name. The song, *Alfie,* from which the quotes in this poem are taken was written by Burt Bacharach and Hal David.

JAMES CASEY

Lone Star Lonely No More

The lone star flies!
Furiously it flies over floodwaters
Harvey rains down from heaven above,
Ferocious breath breathing, beating, brazenly,
As if Satan unleashed the fury of Hell
On that flag.

Solid, the sole star stands.
For solidarity, it stands,
Very soul of Texans united in crisis,
Blue for loyalty, white purity, red bravery
On that flag.

That lone star flies.
In the face of devastation flies,
Flies arrogantly.
Determined,
Those colors fly,
On that flag.

Harvey, you will not divide us.
With purity of heart we reach out
In Galveston and Houston
With bravery in Rockport
And loyalty to Corpus Christi.
What Greater love is there than this,
That one lay down his life for another?

That's what the man in blue did,
With loyalty and bravery,
With purity of heart,
Responsibility beyond belief
Police Officer Steve Perez gave,
Gave his life for Houston.

Harvey, you took his body.
His soul you could not touch.
Houston now his spirit holds,
A star of Texas,
Invisible for the moment
On that flag.

A galaxy of stars
In the moment of crisis shone.
Boats and trucks they gave.
Selflessly, a Texan Dunkirk made.
They too deserve to be
Shining with stellar brilliance
On that flag.

For the moment,
Stars yet unseen
Surround the lone star
That soul star,
Lonely no more,
Waiting to shine in solidarity,
On that flag.

08/30/2017
1:43 am

Human Spirit

Harvey, you revealed the human spirit,
Highways backed up with pick-up trucks
Pulling boats to rescue through floodwaters
Rich and poor, blacks, whites,
Hispanics, people of all stripes,
Republicans, Democrats too.
Pets were included,
Cats and dogs of course,
Hermit crabs and horses
Rescued by boats and helicopters too.

A woman stretched out on a bridge
Reached into rising water,
Saved bats from drowning.
A woman saved bats,
Mexican free-tailed bats from drowning!

Those heroes did not ask
The nature of your politics,
What country you were from.
Labels did not matter.
They saw deeper,
Beyond the color of your skin,
The value of your humanity;
Beyond species too they saw,
Saw the value of life,
The essential, as it were.

Those heroes acted,
Acted with compassion,
With fire in their hearts
To save, save, save,
To save sacred life.

8/31/2017
11:20 pm

Haiku

talk of brevity
trying to write a haiku
today's offering

9/2/2017
9:15 am

a chill in the air
reading about poetry
both my feet are cold

9/2/2017
9:05 am

wisdom not in talk
sophia does not drink wine
silence is golden

9/2/2017
6:25 pm

still chill in the air
read keats poem to autumn
wisdom falls from trees

9/2/2017
6:39 pm

death barking at you
hope dog does not bite your ass
bark bark at that dog

9/3/2017
11:42 am

ants low tech critters
elaborate structures make
no blueprint to boot

9/6/2017
6:04 pm

with eyes of the soul
behold goodness affirmed
a birth of beauty

9/23/2017
11:46 am

walking wounded
hospitals are full of them
thank God people care

1/10/2018
2:26 pm

snow is on the ground
in the branches of the trees
beautiful white world

2/4/2018
5:39 pm

rules rules and more rules
monastic brand on my soul
time to break a few

2/5/2018
10:45 am

My Daimon

As I slept, my Daimon came to me,
A friendly spirit to offer good counsel,
As the one who spoke to Socrates,
You terrify yourself needlessly, said he.

Why do you give free rein
To those demons of your mind?
Like a riotous mob, they run about
Carrying signs flashing catastrophe.

When that is not enough
They hurl harsh criticism,
Nag you with negativity,
Thoughts that pull you down.

They paint a painful picture bleak to bear.
Not satisfied are they to instill self-doubt,
They play that tape over and over
Till in terror you tremble with despair.

Take charge of your mind,
My Daimon said to me.
You create these demons
With an uncontrolled imagination.

You allow them free rein.
Challenge the negative beasts.
Slay the suffering, choose to see
Your world of beauty beckoning you to be.

9/7/2017
6:39 pm

Creation

Of earth, of stars we are.
Cosmological beings we are.
The Universe itself we are.
Not walking around inside it,
Like hamsters rolling about
Inside a plastic globe,
But it, we are it.

The very stuff of the Universe we are,
As it creates itself in the flow,
Like raindrops on the way to the river,
The river flowing to the sea.

The Universe discovering itself,
Knowing itself, aware of itself,
The very consciousness of itself
Participates in the creation of itself.

We are! We are
The evolution of itself
From the big thunderclap
To the raindrops flowing to the sea
Not yet knowing they are the ocean
Cycling itself over and over.

Along the way molten rock
Spun from the sun
Sings the sound of music,
Consciousness singing songs of love,
Songs of hate too,
While creating the world of tomorrow.

Will we ever learn we are
Raindrops flowing to the sea,
Making it what it will be?
Raindrops flowing to the sea,
We are,
Unaware of our source or destiny.

Separate and apart are we,
Like microbes on an onion layer.
We see the level above
And the level below.
Our world is all we know.
Onion we fail to see.

Earth once molten rock,
Now music it makes.
Let's sing with Haydn
Creation's glory,
Songs of love so joyful
We drown the dirge of hate,
A better world create.

9/12/2017
2:52 pm

Love Remains
For Michael Whelan and Erica Van Acker

September 11 impressed upon us that life is a precious gift.
Sen. Bill Frist

My friend has loved deeply
Been touched deeply
By a love that set his heart on fire
Warmed his life
Ignited awareness

Love forged a diamond in his soul
Freed it to radiate the rainbow of love
Light shining from the mountaintop
Goodness affirmed for the world to see
He stands radiant as a star

Then

Suddenly what seemed solid
Indestructible
Steel and stone
Flesh and bone
Crumbled

Life itself disappeared
Martyred by an ideology of hate
Virulent in the minds of men
Hollow minds empty of love
No remains but dust and ashes

But the flame of love remains

More enduring than steel
More solid than stone
Impervious to hate
In the soul of a man remains
Remains solid the flame of love

My friend's Love
Burns in his heart
Forged permanently
As if by the hand of God
Who fuses with the fire of love
Two souls into one

When the body of one returns to the source
The gift of self remains
My friend carries Love within him
She lives in his heart forever
Death the end of a life
The relationship lives on

9/13/17
11:08 am
Revised
2/3/2018
5:10 pm

What is Life?

What is Life?
A questioned posed,
an interesting question too.
They laughed,
as if a frivolous question.

An interesting response!
I wondered why they laughed.
Perhaps no one had an answer,
myself included.

But it is standing here, life,
doing its thing, living.
Atoms crawled out of the sea
to see what they could see.

Atoms became you and me,
Consciousness wondering,
About what it means to be.

When the lights go out
We return to the earth
from whence we came.
Life goes on, they say.

Someone else sees it,
life flowing,
like a river to the sea,
greater than you and me.

Like a pixel in a video,
we contribute to the image
as it flows on, becoming,
always becoming more.
Without pixels what would it be?

But before the lights go out,
when we stand at the edge looking over
into the darkness of the abyss below,
what do we see?

Is it the terror of nothingness?
Do we create an idol of our fear
And call it God?
Perhaps we see a God of judgment
with a tally sheet keeping score
or a God of love
who hopes to see if we discover
we create who we are
and what it means to be.

Snails, snakes, squirrels, doves, or deer,
no other life seems to care.
That question about the meaning of life
for them does not appear,
but we, atoms with consciousness,
we ask: what does life mean,
as if the answer were out there,
hidden in Nature's labyrinth,
a Holy Grail awaiting discovery
or in the mind of God, a gift revealed to us
and only us.
Those other critters need not know.

In the sound of silence,
if we give silence a chance,
Life speaks to us:
Your question, "what does life mean?"
has no answer waiting for you to receive
if you search for it out there.
Siri even found it odd
to ask an inanimate object that question.

You ask the wrong question, said Life to me.
It is I who query you.
Billions of years atoms have been becoming,
becoming a world unconsciously, until
in the last ten seconds of that Cosmic Year
atoms arranged Adam and Eve.

In the garden with the serpent
and all those trees of knowledge
atoms arranged Adam and Eve.
Consciousness emerged,
minds formed, inseparable from each other,
needing each other and the world they knew.

A Universe aware of the flow
of becoming what it could be,
the interdependence of it all.

Now I, Life, ask you, *Homo Creator,*
life with consciousness:
What meaning do YOU bring to life,
to the ongoing flow of which you are?
That is the question.
What is your vision for the world,
the world you make?

This day the world of tomorrow
is in your hands.
Did you think you were insignificant?

9/18/2017
3:13 pm

Noise

Noise noise noise
Everywhere noise
I see it hear it too
Buy this buy that
This little blue pill
Will increase your...
You may have suicidal thoughts
Your heart could give out
A stroke is possible
If it lasts for four hours
Call your doctor
But it will increase your
Your libido
Your memory
Eat Cheerios breakfast of champions
Drive this macho man
You'll be a champ
It will increase your...
What more could you want

You need this
Over and over and over
You need this stuff
Stuff will fill the hole
Make you whole
Complete
Happy

When you get enough
Enough of this and that
This and that this and that
When you get enough
Enough of this and that
You will fill the hole
The hole deep down inside

Your soul you ask
Have you listened to the sound of silence
Silence silence silence
Have you found silence anywhere
Not the silence of the coward
Not the silence of the crowd
Where silence like a cancer grows
But the silence for your soul
The place where character grows
Where your better angels speak
Speak in the sound of silence
Anywhere silence

In the cloister of your mind
If given but a chance
The words of the prophets
Are whispered in their chants
When you know you have enough
You are truly truly rich

9/20/2017
12:58 pm

JAMES CASEY

A Dream

In my dream a vision came.
An ancient urn, a roadmap of cracks
Perched precariously, awaiting
Dithering dignitaries with drinks
To cast an eye and set it safe
Before it falls fractured on the floor,
Shattered and scattered on the floor,
Dithering dignitaries no more.

A blue white marble floating,
Fragile in vast space,
Swirling clouds of ignorance,
A viral haze of hate, infecting minds
Blinded to creative goodness in their hearts,
Blind to benevolence in the other,
Clutching cultural stories that divide.
Unseen is the underlying unifying web.

A new myth lifts the veil of ignorance,
Opens eyes to a transcendent story:
We are kin, star stuff in process of becoming,
Born with the capacity to love,
Sailing the same ship through space.
In solidarity, eyes open wide,
We can set it safe.
The future of that urn is in our hands.

I awake from the dream trembling.

9/24/2017
10:38 pm

Keys to the Kingdom

The world is at stake!
Will we burn it there
Or build a monument
To the grandeur of humanity?

Innate goodness born in us,
Values of the human spirit
Silent in hearts hidden.
Awake from cultural malaise.

Banish the demons
To darkness deep.
Complicity in complacency
Is our share if we fail to care.

Each a pixel in the picture
We create of tomorrow's world today.
Beauty or despair, heaven or hell?
The key to salvation is in our hands.

9/26/2017
1:04 pm

The Word of The Lord

I could hear the Lord
shouting back at you,
an echo up here:
"Why are you trudging all over
looking for me?
Can't you see I'm here,
I'm right here under your feet?
I'm the mountain down under,
down under your feet.

"I gave you eyes to see
no distinctions are necessary.
This is just me,
so look and see.
You may even see your reflection there,
Though no distinctions are necessary.
And when you hear the wind
whisper in the trees,
just wonder
and you will see
it's me.
I am speaking to you right here."

10/16/2017
10:32 am

The Face of Storm King Mountain

Scars mark your face
Glacial scars speak an encounter
With icy forces that shaved
And scarred the sheer side
Of your granite face

An ancient facade
Gnarled in time
Marked by man too
Age has worked
Worked its wonder on you

Your grey crags
Against a blue sky
Composition of beauty
Rise up with majesty
From murky Hudson waters

Waters rushing to the sea
Swift silent softness consuming
Your granite solidity
An ancient face of eternal grace
Soothes as I sit by this river in serenity

10/18/2017
3:00 pm

Mary

Mary, Mary, oh so true
As beautiful as the garden grew.
A flourishing field flowering
Ten thousand shades
Of red, yellow, and blue,
A sparkling diamond beaming
In the glory of the morning dew.

The Robin Returns

Quite a sudden delight!
The robin returned again.
Roused with excitement
To look, watch, and wonder,
I wondered could it be
The same robin that came
In spring to visit me.

Perched on the deck rail as before,
It cocked its head and looked about.
I wondered if it noticed at all,
Leaves curled up brown
Were getting ready for the fall
Or did it come to say farewell
Before white of winter covered all?

11/02/2017
4:45 pm

Trees

Trees speak to me.
In my youth I climbed them, hugged them.
Like a child clinging in maternal arms,
Their branches embraced me.
I remember some as if they were kin.

Trees speak to me
When in silence I am willing to listen.
Their voice, silent as a cloister,
Invites me to deeper silence,
To let go of noise in a distracted mind

And yield to wonder of irrepressible life.
Trees lustily lush as they reach for the sun,
Sun's energy that warms, feeds, fuels us all.
They speak of beauty freely given,
Ten thousand shades of sun dappled green.

In autumn they speak of waning years of life
Still filled with vivid colors, red, yellow, gold.
They remind me of the gifts we bring
To all with eyes to see as leaves hang on
Before they yield to nature's call to fall.

In winter's gray desolation of loss
Trees speak of cold death
As leaves lay on the ground waiting
For earth to return them to the source,
The source from which they came.

Those trees remind me
They and I are kin.
Stuff of the earth we are.
Out of it we came
To it we shall return.

REFLECTIONS ALONG THE WAY

In spring, trees speak to me of joy.
Earth asserts herself
In a conjugal bond with the sun
And in connubial bliss brings forth life,
Replaces the gray of winter's loss.

Ten thousand shades of green
Remind me of vibrant life
Of peace and compassion too
When in summer I sit beneath them
Shade-sheltered from sun's eager energy.

In my reverence for them, I am not alone.
I remember a remnant of Lenni Lenape
Returned each summer in a powwow
To dance around the Tulip Tree
Where the Dutch gypped them of the Island.

Like the Lenni Lenape, I respond
With a song in my heart for trees,
The crisp clear sound of Kathleen Battle
Singing *Exultate Jubilate*.
I am grateful for gratuitous gifts given.

11/08/2017
5:35 pm
Revised
12/10/2017
12:03 pm

The Hermit in Silence Sits

In silence the hermit sits by the river
Contemplating the flow of water
As it cuts through the mountain
Lost in the flow his bag of skin and bones
Rides the waves on the way to the sea

Left behind like emptiness floating in the wind
His self contemplates the not-self
And watches the mountain and river merge
Until all boundaries fade to a larger Self
Self in a bag of skin a convenient illusion

As self realizes Self
He writes a grander story
Than parochial myths that serve to separate
It informs humanity of who it is
And what it means to be

11/25/2017
1:04 pm

Self

You've got to find yourself.
Take time off,
Go in search of yourself,
Travel to foreign lands.

I hear this now and then,
Advice to the young
By a tribal elder.
And wonder what self?

More tribal elders than tribes
Assume they have found it.
But how did it get lost?
Where would it hide itself?

Is this self a treasure chest
Buried on some desolate island?
Can it be found in a bag of skin
Stuffed alongside rib bones?

Which self is searching for it-self?
Is this self a thing to find?

12/06/2017

Self a Dream

The sand was soft as I landed on the beach.
A scruffy old man in rags looked up from
digging.

What are you doing on this isolated island?

I'm searching for a hidden treasure,
For a long time too, as you can see.

How did you get here, I wondered aloud?

In your dream you imagined your self lost, said he.

That's because I was told
By a wise old celebrity,
You have to find yourself.
Take time off.
Travel to foreign lands.
Go in search of yourself.

Well then, here I am
Still searching for the treasure,
Self, an elusive beggar who has so far eluded me.

But you are a figment of my imagination,
You and your illusive self.
Could it be you have no self to find?
Or perhaps you have many selves,
In the community room of your mind,
Kind of like a social entity,
An employee self,
A spouse self,
A friend self,
A child self,
A parent self,
A competent self,

An incompetent self,
A courageous self,
A coward self,
A writer self,
Selves clamoring for ascendancy
And you, at any one time,
The mask of the ascendant self.

Ah, yes, a writer self!
You are writing a story
By choices made,
The narrative of who you are,
A tale you tell yourself moment to moment,
Not fixed in stone, but edited along the way
A story creating a self until it is finished.
And even then the story carries on.

In your dream you imagined your self lost
And have me here digging.
Now, you can imagine there was no self to lose,
I'll stop digging, let you wake up,
Wake up to write your script
Like an unfinished film flowing along,
Your creation of the vision you wish to see.

12/07/2017
10:11 am

JAMES CASEY

On Solitude

Vital spirits flee on autumn winds,
Leave trees bare as bones,
Dark grey bones, stand tall.
The distant mountain through the skeleton
Seen solid against the stark grey sky.

I am glad to see the mountain again,
Though I'll miss the many colors
And warmth of summer and fall.
It reminds me of monastic days,
Walking meditation in silence.

Monks with heads bowed listening
For the silent voice of God
To speak to them of peace on earth
And for the moment peace there was
Beneath silent steadfast mountains.

Mountains standing solid over river waters
Gently carving their way to the sea.
Trees, rocks, river, and mountains
All freed to speak with inner spirits,
A dialogue without distraction.

My mountain today triggers images.
I see Merton on his hermitage patio
Looking out over fields to distant hills
In fertile solitude listening,
Listening to silent voices rise up

From field, forest, and mountain,
As they do for me in silence
Speak of peace and contentment,
And allow wonder at the questions
Inner voices query in quite solitude.

I enjoy the solitude of the forest,
Nature's gentle gift where
Distractions of everyday living
Float away with worldly concerns,
The murderous din of materialism silenced 48

By the sound of stress taking flight,
Evil spirits fleeing the sound of silence,
Fleeing in search of hollow bodies
Plugged into cell phones
In a compulsive connectivity.

Souls without inner solitude,
Self lacking intimacy with self
Searching, searching, searching,
Searching for intimacy anywhere,
Somewhere out there, out there.

When society is made up of men who know no interior solitude it can no longer be held together by love: and consequently it is held together by a violent and abusive authority. Thomas Merton 49

12/20/2017
11:57 am

---

48 Merton, Thomas. *Thoughts in Solitude*. Farrar, Straus and Giroux, 1999, p. xi.
49 Ibid p. xii.

Ancestral Ghosts Exorcised

In solitude, I risk the absence of noise,
Shut the door to unnecessary distractions,
Give myself time to exorcise ancestral ghosts,
Not yet incarnated spirits of the future too
Who haunt the corridors of my mind.

Ancestral spirits fettered
To stories sold generation to generation.
Spirits of my own creation too
Who have elaborated ancestral themes,
To keep telling told tales.

These ghosts remember stories
Of failure, inadequacy, and inability.
Rarely do they sing songs of celebration.
They want to tell me who I am,
Brand me a self-image I cannot escape.

They would have me live a fabricated world,
One of their own inheritance and perpetuation,
Shared by hucksters of commercialization,
In a cave with complicit prisoners celebrating
A worldview of shadows on the wall.

In solitude I risk discovering myself.
I can refuse to entertain ghosts of yore
By watching their attempts to hold on,
Then letting them go like fish on a line
To swim still in the depths of my mind.

I have exposed them to the light,
Countered them by inviting the Muses
To play their arts.
I sing in celebration with those spirits of song.
In silence create a world of beauty.
12/19/2017 3:07 pm

Contrasting Stories at Christmas

Frazzled, that's it, that's the word.
The sound of it captures the feeling
How a shirt must feel when weave
Breaks free and starts to fray.
Loose threads threaten its integrity
As the shirt unravels thread by thread.

This time of year the shirt unravels.
A tapestry of song, glitter, and Santa too
Entice shoppers with Christmas sales
To shop and shop until they drop.
I can't help but feel the frenzy
Until I realize I've bought the story.

Two stories converge in conflict
To tell us who we are.
An ancient story
Inspires human meaning.
The more recent,
Informs emptiness within.

The child born a light to the world
With angels song of hope for all,
Peace on the earth good will to men.
The story, each child of innocence born
With the capacity of love for all,
In solidarity can create a beneficent world.

Today, at birth, a different story told.
Welcome to the world of consumerism.
It is the matrix of human life.
You are not OK, so BORN TO SHOP you are.
Filling the hole with stuff makes you whole.
He who dies with the most toys wins.

12/21/2017 02:01 pm

JAMES CASEY

Christmas Story

In the silence of the night
The birth cry of a child
Born in a simple stable
Pierces the darkness
With a burst of light.

The story of this child,
Love incarnate born,
Arms open wide to the world,
Eager to embrace another,
Is the story of every child at birth.

All life is good says this story,
Lambs and lions,
Goats and gadflies too,
Seen from God's point of view.

Strange how we see life,
Divide it up then rate it,
With a skewed perspective
Our own point of view,
As if ours was a God's eye view.

Cultural stories all across the world
Passed down from primordial times
Speak of specialness that serves to separate.
Will we ever transcend stories that divide
To see we are kin of the same stuff made?

Born with arms open wide to the world,
As the child of old, eager to embrace another,
Can we with knowledge of the cosmos found,
Create a love story in time to save us all?

12/24/2017
11:01 am

L'Histoire de Noël

Dans le silence de la nuit
Le cri de naissance d'un enfant
Né dans une écurie simple
Perce l'obscurité
Avec un éclat de lumière.

L'histoire de cet enfant,
L'amour incarné né,
Les bras s'ouvrent largement sur le monde,
Désireux d'en embrasser un autre,
C'est l'histoire de chaque enfant à la naissance.

Toute la vie c'est bonne dit cette histoire,
Agneaux et lions,
Chèvres et taons aussi,
Vu du point de vue de Dieu.

Étrange comment nous voyons la vie,
Divisons-la, puis évaluons-la,
Avec une perspective biaisée
Notre propre point de vue,
Comme si notre vision était celle de Dieu.

Histoires culturelles partout dans le monde
Transmis des temps primordiaux
Parlez de la particularité qui sert à séparer.
Saurons-nous jamais transcender les histoires
qui divisent
Pour voir que nous sommes des parents de la
même chose faite?

Né avec les bras grands ouverts sur le monde,
Comme l'enfant d'autrefois, désireux d'en
embrasser un autre,
Pouvons-nous avec bien connaître du cosmos
trouvé,
Créer une histoire d'amour à temps pour nous
sauver tous?

Lonely

Alone
Is
Lonely

Only

If
I
Think so

Creative spirits
Manifest
In the café of my mind

And like Camus and Sartre
At *Les Deux Magots*
I imbibe with them

Till spirits liberate
In fertile dialogue
My creative self

1/6/2018
1:43 pm
Revised
2/2/2018
10:06 am

Something Big

Something big is going on here,
Really big, right here, everywhere,
In me, in you too,
In here, out there.

I need silence to see it,
To be caught by the wonder,
Feel the awe, that awful feeling.
My arms open wide to embrace it,

To bring it into my heart
Left speechless,
Feelings fumbling for words.
It is awesome, just awesome.

In the dark night
On this marble-in-the-sky
I look out as starlight penetrates,
Throttles me with wonder

About stars,
Light I see and light I don't;
How it gets from there to here,
The distance it travels, time too.

I see light,
Call it a star.
Is it still there or did it die,
Die long ago that I might live?

If I could get outside all of this,
Look at it as a time-lapse film
From the speck at the Bang
Till this momentary immensity,

It would be awful,
Speechless feelings
Fumbling for words.
Wonderful, just awesome!

1/13/2018
11:14 am

Alone

Alone
The mirror of the heart
Reflects spirits
I listen
Know them

Challenge
Forgive
Free
Fortify some
Deny none

The door open
Wonder enters
Visions and questions
Enrich the inner dialogue
Of whom I choose to become

With compassion
Patience
Spirits sing songs of love

I compose an unfinished symphony
In my mind
Enriched by wonders I let in
Songs of spirits
In silence I alone hear

The music created
In love with spirits of my soul
Is an invitation to sing.

1/7/2018
10:09 am

Awesome

Awesome,
That word so abused,
Until I stand in the center
Of the Cathedral of Chartres
Or the Sistine Chapel and know,

Know the awful feeling
Of being filled with awe
Like medieval architects
Compelled to create cathedrals,
Michelangelo to paint creation.

The world is my cathedral,
The night sky painting
The unfinished tableau of creation.
I stand amidst the stars
On a speck of the Universe,

A speck looking at itself in awe.
I see stars embraced by darkness
And wonder about light,
Specks of light that reach out
And touch me from afar.

I feel something big flowing on here
Greater than you and I,
But we are it, in the flow,
A small speck on a speck
With something to say.

Awesome!

1/12/2018
3:23 pm

The World We Think We Know

Fish swimming in a pond
Contribute to the water
The pollution all suck in
No complaint about quality
It is the world they know

We like fish
Swim in toxicity
Float in complacency
Suck in the crap others dole out
It is the world we know

One day a fish risks life
Jumps out of the water
Sees a world of delight
Back in the pond it explains
To floaters in toxicity who know

They know they know
All agree they know
They know how to ridicule
You hear the chuckle on nightly news
As they confabulate with one another

1/23/2018
12:58 pm

Snow Fall

Ah! Here it is
Snow again
Coming down
From heaven above
To whiten the world
As if to purify
The soiled remnant
From the last fall

I watch snowflakes fall
Large slow flakes
Six-sided shapes
In fine frail form
Form a delicate lace
To beautify my world
With wondrous grace
That covers all

Flakes fall
Each separate
All unique
Yet on the ground
Unique transforms
In solidarity to form
A snow-white blanket
Over all

I wonder about the world
Is it filled with flakes
Unique stories of their own
Unwilling to transcend
To form in solidarity a new story
With wondrous grace
A delicate lace
To save us all
2/7/2018 5:24 pm

Seed to Soul

Energy contained
Like the heart of a seed
In inner turmoil straining
Impatient for transformation
Flashes forth with nowhere to flow
A big bang according to Hoyle
A name of derision he meant

Inflation from within
Expanding the point
Not an explosion in space
But an expansion of space
From God knows what
Into somethingness
Lumpy energy in waves

Waves unevenly spread
Within a space
Freshly fabricated
Flowing toward infinity
Forced together by an enactment
Goldilocks would find just right
Thank God for that

For if not
Then not this
This bag of atoms
Atoms with consciousness
Here writing
Wondering
Whence this law of attraction

On some day
Actually no day
There are no days yet
A great light burst forth
A sun was born burning
Birth that brought forth life
Life from star death did come

First fusion forms new form
A thorough transformation
In which element begets element
Until elemental food
Forms from Sun's energy
To feed us all
Who from the sea did crawl

The energy of the Sun
From the sea did crawl
To form the world
We know today
It took awhile
But here we are
Souls from suns

I wonder about souls
Are we souls with soul
Like soul singing souls
Or Faustian souls
Who've sold out their souls
And what about tomorrow
Will a great light burst forth

2/12/2018
2:23 pm

JAMES CASEY

Rachel Weeping For Her Children

"My heart is broken
Our world is shattered,"
The word of a father fractured,
"Where do I go from here?"

Beautiful people
Smiling with life, alive,
Then in terror terminated,
Life, precious life, terminated.

The world is shattered!

I hear a father's despair,
Grief incarnate.
Feel it in my gut
And I know, I know

The world is shattered.
        SHATTERED
The world is shattered.

How long will Rachel
Have to weep for her children,
Her children who are no more? 50
How long, oh God, how long?

The world is shattered!

Our world is shattered.
We bring children into this world,
The world of our creation.
It is a world of our making.

---

50 See Jer 31:15 and Mt 2:18 "Rachel weeping for her children,
and refusing consolation, because they are no more."

144

How long will Rachel
Have to weep for her children?
How long will we fail to see,
To see the world we make?

This shattered world!

"Fly with the angels"
My loves, my doves,
My beautiful ones,
"I will forever remember you,

My sweet angel."
"In Paradisum deducant te Angeli…"[51]
May the angels lead you
Lead you into Paradise.

But in Rachel's weeping heart,
Burning you will remain.
The fire of love eternal
Alive in the hearts you loved.

2/17/2018
3:52 pm

---

51 *In Paradisum* is a hymn sung at end of the traditional Latin
Requiem Mass of the Roman Catholic Church. It is sung in
Gregorian Chant. The English translation is: "May the Angels
lead you into paradise: may the martyrs receive you at your
coming, and lead you into the holy city, Jerusalem. May the choir
of Angels receive you, and with Lazarus, who once was poor,
may you have everlasting rest."

I Wonder About The World

I wonder about the world,
The human created one.
I remember the ancient sage reminded us
The power of choice is in our hand:
To each of us is given
The key to the Kingdom of Heaven
The same key opens the Gates of Hell.

I think about Dante's *Inferno*,
Man's sins against neighbor
And Hell for Sartre, is other people.
I am reminded of Camus' novel, *The Fall*:
We don't need God to create Hell.
Our fellow men do that quite well
With our help, of course.

I wonder today, is there a story about
As if told by Satan himself
Where yet our fellow men suffice?
A story told not like prophets of old
Who spoke for the soul
Of love of neighbor, justice for all
As the key to Paradise?

Are the prophets of this day men of greed
Who would have us believe
It is all about us and the stuff we need
To fill the hole in the soul,
The emptiness within?
Is the message of salvation,
He who dies with the most toys wins?

Is that the key to Paradise
They would have us believe?
Getting the stuff, is it ever enough
Or is it like chasing the will-o'-the-wisp,

An endless search for the Garden of Eden
Along a foggy road to nowhere
Where the street sign reads: Dead End?

I wonder about another story
Where Big Brother and his cousin Big Data
Who collude with Corporate Man,
All eager for control, could play no role
In what to believe or what we need.
Is there time yet with the key in my hand
To find the way to the Garden of Eden?

I can call on my muses to let me see
The garden of my own spirituality
In which I get to sing songs of fraternity,
Dance creativity with my brothers and sisters
And sculpt in the garden ten thousand flowers,
Fields of fruit trees, bright blossoms of color,
While together we celebrate one another.

This is not yet a rose garden in bloom,
For in my dreams flowers flourish
My muses indeed will to dance.
In practice, love is difficult, demanding.
Weeds spontaneous sprout. Some set strong.
With weak hands the row is hard to hoe,
But together with another I can weed and sow,

Sow seeds of love with help from others.
Imagine the garden of love we can grow
With that key to Paradise in our hand.

2/28/2018
5:21 pm
Revised
3/5/2018
2:47 pm

What Have We Done To The Spirit

Like virgin snow gentle on the ground
Without a mark to abuse the beauty
We are born a gift the world gifts itself
Waiting to unwrap the goodness we bring

The crocus pierces spring snow a jewel of joy
Each child a precious gem born of the earth
A bud bursting with potential energy
Creative spirit waiting to flower our world

For we are born arms open wide
Willing to embrace the other
We are burning embers of love
Ready to set the world on fire

A fire of a different kind
Now consumes the land
What have we done to the spirit
And where have all the flowers gone

Commentary

This poem was written as a result of the tragedy at
Marjory Stoneman Douglas High School in Parkland,
Florida on February 14, 2018 where 17 children were
killed. The poem is meant to celebrate the creative
potential each child is born with at birth to make this a
more beautiful world, but it also raises the question
about what we as a culture have done to impede that
potential from achieving full bloom.

2/22/2018
6:10 pm

What Beautiful Snow Can Do

Snow, gentle beautiful snow
Covers the sins of the world,
The world I can see.
This world purified,
Dressed in pure white,
As if the Heavenly Hosts
Spread perfectly white wings over the land.

Everything white, pure white,
Just a hint of dark grey to let us know
The trees are still there.
Hemlocks stand tall, adorned in white gowns,
No suggestion of green in outstretched arms.
They are bowed in adoration, as are all trees,
Every branch dressed in pure white.

The sky forms a dull white backdrop
To this brilliant world below
Where there is no electricity,
Neither heat nor running water,
No Internet, the phone is dead.
The world has stopped,
Given us a pause to reflect in silent solitude,

Not for everyone, though.

A mother weeps for a child lost.
A tree could no longer bear the weight.
I think of the mother and the child taken.
Grief, unbearable grief!
I'm reminded of Puerto Rico,
People abandoned to the Stone Age.

What have I done to help?
The lights are back on. The heat is coming up.
Will I take it all for granted again?

Love Mountain

In the dream, love is like a mountain
Grown out of the river below.
I see two eagles spiral upward,
Buoyed by warm air beneath their wings.
They soar to the heights like Blue Angels
Then tumble through the sky in free-fall,
Talons locked as they cartwheel together,
Confidant in courtship play.

But awake, love is a mountain.
From a distance, it seduces,
A glorious invitation to ecstasy.
Closer, it whispers euphoria.
Wind beneath outstretched wings
Lets the eagle soar on high.
While on the ground, the climb varies.
Views vitalize while boulders and cliffs await.

At the trailhead, a warning sign.
To climb this mountain:
   Know yourself
   Take responsibility
   Reduce expectations
   Affirm the other
   Give all to reach the top.
Together the climb is so much the better.

It begins a gentle path,
Slight ups and downs along the forest floor
Where the sweet smell of hemlock pervades
And penetrates the soul, a perennial reminder
To love oneself is a present for the other.

In time, the climb steepens.
Roots and rocks on which to trip
Abound along the way,
A challenge to the hike ahead,
But I look at them with care,
For flowers may be hidden there
That will brighten my day
If only I will choose to see.

There are joys along the way,
On the way to the top
To celebrate the world view
Where together we can see
The world holding us
Like two diamonds in its hand
And in delight know
We are the dance of dazzling light.

We dance it, dazzling light, for all to see
Two eagles, talons locked in trust,
As we cartwheel through the sky
With all the risks love imposes
And let the brightness of the light
Radiate through our world.
Like the energy of the sun it will warm all,
This bond of love we have created.

3/27/2018
5:13 pm
Revised
3/31/2018
6:18 pm

Gratitude

I'm glad **to be** here.
I can **see**.
I see a blue sky, sparing spring clouds,
With clean white snow still around.
I **know**.
I know spring will soon be here.
Knowing I know, how wonderful is that,
When I see all around me here
Not-knowing like that!
I can even **foresee** what may become,
Like spring daffodils yellow and white.

The source of all is the same
For me and that which is around.
Yet, from only some of that primal stuff,
Consciousness did emerge.
And here it is **writing** a poem,
The result of a long slow process,
The poem and the consciousness.
And in me, the **material stuff**
All arranged well enough
To **speak** words, like long and enough, that
Symbolize a **thought** emerged from where?

I am **grateful** for all that,
And the **reason** I have, to take **delight**
In what I **learn** from the past
And store in the mystery of **memory**,
Food to feed an **imagination**.
Now that is another mystery,
Which enables me to **create**
Gifts of beauty for others to enjoy.
A lot in the pot to be thankful for.

3/15/2018
6:15 pm

A Spring Greeting

I open the door to see snow,
Still snow on the ground
Where I long to see green grass.
In sudden surprise, I spy green spikes,
Straight, sharp, impatient, green spikes,
A resurrection of daffodils, pierce the snow

While yet another surprise greets me.
Huite huite, huite huite huite huite huite,
Chigua chigua chigua chigua chigua chigua.
I see it standing straight, in sharp silhouette
A shock of red in stunning contrast,
Proud, bright, among green hemlocks.

My first cardinal of the season,
Sings a spring serenade.
I am delighted to hear the cheerful song,
Crisp and clear to dampened ears
Slowly silenced by age, sound enough still
To delight in the sound of joy.

I prefer to think he greets me
Than know he warns his mate
Of this intruder in their world.
It is a much more pleasant welcome
Than the rapid raspy caw caw caw
Of the congress of crows as I open up the door.

They delight me too, though,
Just to know the connection
And to think they are as glad
To announce my appearance
As I am to hear them.
I thank them with silence.

3/29/2018 5:58 pm

153

God Doesn't Draw Straight Lines

God doesn't draw with straight lines.
Mountains beckon me. I want to climb them,
though it is difficult for me, always difficult
and now I feel that day may be done.

A tinge of sadness affects me when I see one
now and know it calls out to me in vain.
I am glad nonetheless that they surround me.
I see mountains every day.

They lift up my heart. I enjoy their company.
I am blessed to live within their beauty
and am even more blessed with their beauty,
which lives in me.

They constantly compel me to reflect,
to reflect on God and straight lines.
Man likes straight lines, makes things with
them, wants to square things up, not God,
thank God.

God draws like a child, squiggly lines,
lots of ups and downs.
I drive amongst them, alongside them.
They inspire my trip, challenge me
to be grateful, never forget.

How could I forget to realize
I am privileged to live amongst them?
On top of them, when I've finally made it there
I am overwhelmed with awe, wonder, majesty.

Gerard Manley Hopkins got it right
whether you believe in God or not.
On top of a mountain you know,
you feel it in your bones, "The world is
charged with the grandeur of God." 52

4/1/2018
10:33 pm

---

52 This is the first line of the poem, "God's Grandeur," by Gerard
Manley Hopkins, from my high school memory.

A Stellar Development

For Brian, James, and Patrick

Persons grow out of the ground
Australian Aboriginals say.
They suffer by being somewhere else.
I think the Aboriginals got it right.

We are of the Earth, earthy.
We have come out of the Earth
and to it we shall return. At times,
along the way, we suffer not being here.

Carl Sagan said we are star stuff.
All elements that make up our bodies
and the planets were forged inside of stars.
We are even now connected to stars.

The Sun sends us energy, warms us,
feeds plants that feed the animals that we eat.
We are the energy of the Sun incarnated
with consciousness, a stellar development.

In solitude, with a mind not distracted,
I get to enjoy the wonder of it all,
as I realize the revelation is reality.
I am not anything small and insignificant.

I am the stuff of the Universe,
the Universe doing its thing.
And that stuff, with its consciousness,
participates in creating the world of tomorrow.

I am a creator, a cosmological being
once thought of as isolated, separated.
Something to be said for stepping outside
the polluted pond, the culture of delusion,

and in solitude, seeing the world
and myself for what I am,
part of the unfolding process of creation.
Out of the process emerged this consciousness.

Consciousness of the Universe is who I am,
star stuff that thinks, reflects, learns, creates.
I can pass on what I have learned to others,
a link in the growing chain of knowledge.

That link fueled by energy, energy of the Sun,
itself a link in the chain back to the Big Bang.
It feeds my life to create order from chaos
in the Universe disorder bound.

I can plant seeds to grow a vegetable garden
and with spark sow seminal seeds to procreate,
a son from the energy of the Sun, a wonder,
whose sons may return to stars seeds of life.

Imagine, consciousness sprouts on exoplanets,
looks out across the vastness of space,
wonders how it got there, and asks itself:
is there any purpose in the Universe?

With you right here and now,
atoms of the Earth, once desolate rock,
together in chorus sing songs of aspiration,
to even serenade stars that we are on our way.

Cosmological beings continue creation,
star stuff on the return trip to the stars,
an astronomical journey for humanity.
A stellar development, indeed!

4/23/2018
11:35 am

TESS [53]

TESS is on her way.
She set sail yesterday evening for
A two year journey of adventure
To see what no one has seen.

As in a child's dream of other worlds,
she'll pass through the arch of experience
to see what hides beyond the horizon
as she sets her sight on untraveled worlds

in search of obscure knowledge
that she will now bring to light.
She'll take pictures of what she sees
with eyes of human ingenuity made

to show us what we cannot see,
a place of human hope to find
with rocks and water and enough stuff
for life to live or soil to grow.

On this trip, TESS takes us
a step closer to the stars
to see if there is life out there
or the elements that will let it grow.

Someday, we will return to the stars
to spread the seeds of sentience,
the ongoing flow of fecund creation
that can imagine a universe lush with life.

4/20/2018 8:10 pm

---

53 TESS is the acronym for Transiting Exoplanet Survey
Satellite, NASA's search for planets, called exoplanets, around
neighboring suns. It launched on 4/18/2018 at 6:51 pm.

Firefighters Obey The Highest Law

For Fireman Francis Xavier Casey, Engine 18 NYFD, RIP

True to life they are
True to death they lie
Like Spartans at Thermopylae
In obedience to the highest law 54

One of which they never speak
Nor is it ordered by another
For love burns in the heart
And is supported by each other

A brotherhood of valor
Firefighters rush to hell
Where no man would dare to go
There are men like that women now too

Who leave self on the ground
Climb the ladder to save a mother
To pull her from the fire
Then go back in to save another

Rough men gruff men they are
Down to earth boisterous men
A tough shell may hide compassion
But a soft soul resides inside

I knew several men like that
One who spoke a thousand words
With a simple touch on my head
It imprinted love in my heart

---

54 "The highest law" – see John 15:12,13, "This is my commandment: love one another, as I have loved you. A man can have no greater love than to lay down his life for his friends."

This fireman answered his final call
Like the 300 at Thermopylae
In answer to the highest law
Laid down his life for love of all

4/24/2018
1:04 pm

Convenient Labels

Boxes, boxes, let's put people in boxes.
I can put myself in there too.
It's convenient to my way of thinking.
I don't have to think at all.
How efficient is that!

The world becomes colorless,
Well not quite.
Black and white will do.
So I live in a world without hue
And without hue, I am hueless.

But I do need you.
After all, if your agenda suits me,
I wear a coat of armor.
And the chain of simplicity binds,
So I am certainly not clueless.

And I know who you are.
We share the same label.
It works.
I feel good.
We are *compañeros, los otros, combatientes.*

There are guys on street corners,
You find them in churches too,
selling identity labels.
You are good, you are bad, you are ugly so.
It is easy for the indigent to buy a few.

Especially when they all agree it fits you.
But I wonder, where have all the colors gone?
Ah, they are over there, in the box labeled,
"Independent Thinking."
Could that be Pandora's box?

The Demilitarized Zone

I saw them standing there,
faces with smiles radiant it appeared,
standing there in the demilitarized zone,
standing straight together.
Their arms embraced a boy and girl.

I couldn't but wonder about the light,
would it go on to enlighten the world,
not the flash of a nuclear blast,
but Sophia's light, the light of life.
Would the wisdom of children

flow through their arms to destroy
the nuclear bombs
that would annihilate those children at play?
The children are shields of light
who radiate bright the innocence of life.

Powerful prophets who utter not a word,
shine a bright light on the way we were born.
They stand in front of those men with arms, 55
speak of gentleness, beauty, and hope for life
without harm where the lights will go on 56.

4/28/2018
12:13 pm

---

55 "Those men with arms" are President Moon Jae-in of South Korea and President Kim Jong-un of North Korea.
56 The reference to the lights is meant to suggest both wisdom and an improved quality of life in the North. North Korea seen from space at night is dark in comparison to South Korea.

ACKNOWLEDGEMENTS

I wish to express my gratitude for my mother and father who instilled in me values that have informed my life. I was blessed to have my grandmother in my life everyday as a child, as well. She affirmed me with love and wisdom. My family passed on to me the stories they inherited along with the foibles of ancestral spirits that have challenged me along the way to confront the story, do my bit to polish it up, and pass it on.

I am grateful to my two adult children for the joy they continue to bring into my life and that they don't remind me daily that I could have polished up my part of the story a bit more. I know it and ask their forgiveness.

I hope I pass on to them the wisdom that they can edit the stories they have inherited, release the chains that bind, open the cage and let their spirits fly free to sing songs of joy and wonder. They are precious gems, gifts to the world, as are the two most recent gems, grandsons James and Patrick who have been filling my world with the sound of music, songs joy, pure delight.

I was fortunate to enter another family along the way, the Brothers of the Christian Schools, a religious order in the Roman Catholic Church. They provided me with a most wholesome environment of wonderful, committed Brothers with whom I lived and worked, models of inspiration. They helped me to understand that life is fulfilled in service to others.

I am grateful to the Mahopac Library Writers Group, the Mahopac Poetry Workshop, and the Yorktown Poetry Group for the assistance they have provided me. I want to thank Michael Whelan and Dennis Sullivan, both poets who read the manuscript and offered suggestions.

ABOUT THE AUTHOR

James Casey, born in New York City, grew up at the northern tip of Manhattan Island. After teaching high school as a member of a Catholic religious order followed by a career in the justice system, he returned as an adjunct professor to teach religion and philosophy at Manhattan and Marist colleges. He holds a Master Degree in Pastoral Counseling from Iona College and a Master Degree in Theology from Manhattan College.

A proud achievement is the reacquisition and preservation of stained glass windows that were in the former novitiate of the Brothers of the Christian Schools. They are now installed in the chapel at Manhattan College, Bronx, NY.

For many years he hiked and skied in the High Peaks of the Adirondack Mountains and hiked the mountains of the Hudson Highlands, in Putnam County, New York where he lives. He raised his two children there with his wife Barbara and now enjoys visits from his grandchildren, as well as the deer and birds that tolerate him as a guest in their territory.

1121

Made in the USA
Columbia, SC
12 May 2018